Further Issues and Challenges

For Consideration, Discussion And Consensus.

Peter C. Bruechle

Copyright 2022 © Peter C. Bruechle
All rights reserved. This book or any portion thereof may not be reproduced or used in any manner whatsoever without the express written permission of the publisher except for the use of brief quotations in a book review.

ISBN 978-0-6450839-4-1

Set in Times New Roman

I thank all the people who have helped me with the writing of this short book.

My special thanks to my wife Kaye for her support and help, and to Tony Brand for his thoughts and opinions during discussions, and for his long time friendship.

My thanks also to my sons Nicholas and Hans – Nick for his invaluable help with getting "Issues" into its final state and Hans for his production of the cover.

Contents

Preface 6

1. The Importance Of Selecting Qualified Leaders 8

2. Humanity's Rises, Falls, And Future Possibilities. 24

3. The Importance Of Us 29

4. Giving Or Taking? 33

5. War And/Or Peace 1 38

6. War And/Or Peace 2 40

7. Global Warming / Climate Change – A Reprise. 46

8. Another View Of Global Warming. 56

9. Comparing Possible Future Electrical Power Sources.... 60

10. Future Aims For Humanity. 77

11. Questions For Our Time... 82

PREFACE.

This addition to my earlier book "Issues and Challenges" has been written as a basis for discussion on matters I regard as weaknesses in the psychological make-up of humans. There are questions with no answers, such as why humanity considers itself so important when in the great scheme of things it is not important at all. The strong and able should realise this and should be humble and strive to build a better and fairer world – not attempt to dominate other humans. Why is humanity's nature such that we continuing to fight with each other, killing and maiming, when there are massive challenges for humanity that need investigation. Examples are:

- Why does humanity not work together to overcome the many problems of our world and to solve its many mysteries?
- Why do we go on arguing, fighting and killing when the only beneficiaries are the makers of the weapons being used? Is it to relieve the Earth from overcrowding?
- How can humanity be persuaded to use its intelligence – intelligence that sends humans into space and returns them, and controls nuclear energy – to achieve a safer and more comfortable world?

I recognise that my efforts will not lead to the changes that need to be made. I suspect that it will require a destructive holocaust that will result in large proportions of the populations of the Earth – both the animal populations, including we humans, and the vegetable populations – being slaughtered or poisoned, and its production capacity being largely ruined, before humanity realises that none will be winners from such a destructive event.

Despite my pessimism which, given humanity's performance to date, appears to be justifiable, I am still hopeful that we will overcome our ridiculous biases and will realise that humanity either unites, thrives, and lives in balance with the Earth's production capacities as it faces new challenges that will arise, or it will suffer degradation and, possibly, extinction. The alternative is that it continues on with its divisions, its displays of childish greed and it's ridiculous warring, which will result in destruction of much of the product of previous civilisations and the death, and mutilation, of many of us naked apes.

Even if humanity can overcome its current stupidities and acts as a united body, it is likely that it will have many, as yet unknown, challenges to face in the future. If it is to be successful in overcoming these challenges it will require the bulk of the human population to contribute to their societies, and to learn to live in peace and, hopefully, prosperity within the productive capacity of the globe. For this to happen, humanity will need to learn to control some of its basic characteristics – greed, sloth, envy, wrath and excessive pride.

We humans all need to realise that unless we can learn to live together peacefully we could destroy our Earth – our home. Humanity also needs to control the monsters among us who apparently think nothing of destroying the works of humankind and killing others.

1. THE IMPORTANCE OF SELECTING QUALIFIED LEADERS.

Perhaps the most puzzling mystery of humanity's short domination of our planet Earth is why the various groups who make up that humanity have not yet found a way to live peacefully and productively with each other. Surely there are enough challenges for us to conquer without various groups, and persons, attempting to annihilate each other. Why can the various groups not pool their energies and their intelligences into producing positive and peaceful pursuits? Why do the various groups insist on, and delight in, developing more, and more destructive, weapons – weapons that are now so destructive they could extinguish life on our Earth, our one, and only, viable planet? Why does humanity, even quite civilised humanity, give power to warlords instead of to peacemakers?

What is the weakness in the human psyche that leads to the energy and inventiveness that could be used to create a better, more liveable world being, instead, absorbed by stupid and destructive conflicts? The energy, human effort, cost, and intelligence required for conflict could be channelled into benefits for the whole human race and its supporting crops and animals. Why do the various ethnic, religious, and racial groups spend effort on conflict – on domination?

Further Issues and Challenges

Most importantly, why are leadership roles so often filled by those, mainly men (although this is changing), who consider themselves to be superior and who consider their particular tribe or religion to be the only group entitled to lead – even to exist? And why has the bulk of humanity not followed peaceful leaders? Based on the evidence of history, humanity's drives are not peaceful development, but dominance. The list of leaders who have disgraced humanity is long. Examples from the past are:

- *Genghis Khan.* He conquered central Asia and China in the late 12th century and the early 13th century. As he conquered, he killed.
- *Alexander the Great.* He was born in Macedonia in 356BC and amassed the largest empire of the ancient world by pillaging, murder, rape, and arson.
- *Attila the Hun.* He led his Huns from 434AD until his death in 453AD. He sacked and burned Roman cities. His nick name was the Scourge of God.
- *Caligula.* He ruled Rome from 37 AD until 41 AD and led campaigns of sadism, extravagance, and sexual perversion.

Alexander the Great in Egypt. This 'Great' man's campaigns killed over 120,000 people.

More recently the world has been forced to endure such leaders as:

- *Oliver Cromwell.* He treated Catholics appallingly in the 17th century.
- *Pol Pot.* He created a brutal regime in Cambodia. His rule of terror led to the deaths of nearly a quarter of his country's seven million people.

- *Napoleon Bonaparte.* Born in 1769, Napoleon conquered much of Europe after France had recovered from the French Revolution (1789 – 1799). Given that he was responsible for much destruction and for the deaths of so many, it is unclear why he is still revered by many.
- *Adolf Hitler.* (1899 – 1945). He rose from being a corporal in the first World War to lead a resurgent Germany into World War 2. Why the energetic Germans followed him into disaster remains a mystery. It is possible that a part of the reason is that the terms of the settlement that ended the First World war were so harsh that the German people were still smarting from being treated so badly. They wanted to prove they were a master race, and saw Hitler as a leader who could lead them on to their rightful position as a world power. Instead he led them to disaster.
- *Mao Zedong.* Born in 1893, Mao has been accused of being responsible for the deaths of 65 million people.
- *Joseph Stalin.* Born in 1878, Stalin – whose birth name was Joseph Jughashvili – died in 1953. He was a consummate politician and a ruthless thug. He was not a man of peace, and he was responsible for millions of deaths. He believed in power – not in peace.
- *George W. Bush.* Born in 1946 into the family of George H. W. Bush who was President of the USA from 1989 to 1993, George W. Bush became the 43rd President of the USA for the period 2001 to 2009 by the narrowest of margins.

George W's presidency was noted for several unique occurrences and developments. One was the increase in the national debt to $11.3 trillion, which more than doubled the owed amount he inherited in 2000. Others were the tragic attacks on the World Trade Centre on the 11th of September 2001, during which nearly 3000 people were killed and 25,000 were injured, and the simultaneous attack on the Pentagon.

Features of his presidency were America's attack on Afghanistan in October 2001, shortly after the destruction of the World Trade

Further Issues and Challenges

Centre, and the invasion of Iraq in 2003 following America's false belief that Saddam Hussein was developing weapons of mass destruction (WMD). George W. had supporters but was not held in high regard by the bulk of countries of the world.

In 2006, 18 of 21 countries who responded had an unfavourable opinion of the Bush administration and considered it was negative to world security. George W. Bush was a warmonger, not a peacemaker.

Today much of the world is led by leaders of very doubtful worth – leaders who are arming their countries with high powered elements of war, that they say are for "defence". Examples are:

- *Kim Jong-un of North Korea.* He has heavily armed his country with long range ballistic missiles and nuclear submarines *"to defend itself"* against the United States of America. The gain that the USA would achieve from invading North Korea is difficult to find, and how long-range missiles and nuclear submarines, which are weapons of offense, not defence, can be used to defend a country is quite unclear. However, given the USA's penchant for interfering in other countries' squabbles – Vietnam, Afghanistan, Iraq – it is not surprising that Kim has selected it as a most likely aggressor. He is obviously a dangerously fanatical leader with little sense of history or of humanity joining together to peacefully solve the challenges that the world will throw at us. Nothing appears to be further from his mind than a world at peace.

- *Xi Jinping, President of China.* He is the son of a deputy Prime Minister who was a comrade of Mao Zedong, so he was born into political power. Then his father was purged so that Xi Jinping spent several years as a labourer.

  As President he has instructed his forces to ready themselves for war, which they have done. He is, simultaneously, leading the "Belt and Road" initiative that has been described as a state backed plan for global dominance.

Xi appears to be buying important ports, including Darwin, and taking charge of strategic areas, then developing them using Chinese contractors, but at the cost of the sovereign power, who is then indebted to China.

According to Google, the value of contracts awarded to Chinese contractors, in 2017, ($340 billion) far exceeded the expenditure on the "Belt and Road" initiative by China ($210 billion). There are critics who consider that the Belt and Road initiative is economic imperialism, and its real purpose is to provide China with military presences in critical places.

Currently there is concern that Xi will attempt to take the island of Taiwan by force as he considers it belongs to China. This will be resisted by the citizens of Taiwan. How this will play out, whether or not Taiwan will be forced to join China's hegemony, and what the reaction of the western world will be should China attempt to take Taiwan by force, remains to be seen.

There is little doubt that Xi's aims are for China to take the leading position in the future world, and with the energy China is displaying it is likely he will succeed. Whether this is good or bad for the world, including Australia, will unfold in the future. Xi certainly does not appear to have as his main aim a united and peaceful humanity. He appears to want Chinese domination.

- *Bashar al-Assad.* After his father, who was the President of Syria, died in 2000 Bashar's presidency was assured by several powerful groups. He promised reforms that included fighting corruption, forming a democracy, and modernising the economy. Once in power he limited the freedom of the press, had leading opposition figures arrested, and called for referenda, the conduct, and results of which have been criticised by opposition groups. He has continued a war with Israel and has had a running war with so called "rebels" who control areas of his country. The fighting with the rebels has destroyed several Syrian cities. There is no doubt that Bashar al-Assad is not a person who desires peace and productivity.

- *Vladimir Putin.* Putin is frightening. Just what his long-term ambitions are have not been made clear, but from what he has so far managed to get done, which is impressive in many ways, they were not done to achieve world peace. From being a foreign intelligence officer for the KGB (the Committee for State Security) he advanced to being an advisor to Anatoly Sobchak, the first democratically elected mayor of St. Petersburg. He later became deputy mayor.

In 1996 he moved to Moscow and joined the staff of Pavel Borodin, the Kremlin's chief administrator. He was later advanced to the directorship of the FSB (the KGBs successor) by Boris Yeltsin. Yeltsin was seeking an appropriate heir to take his place as President and appointed Putin to the role of Prime Minister in 1996. This was followed by Yeltsin resigning and naming Putin as President. He then won the vote for his presidency in an election in 2000.

All has not been plain sailing with problems arising in the "Silk Road" countries – especially in Crimea and Ukraine. As I write this in April 2022, Putin has established armed forces on Ukraine's border and has attacked Ukraine's inferior armed forces. These are being backed by NATO and other countries but there is no move for the western world to join the action – probably because of their concern that the badly balanced Putin could revert to nuclear weapons. There is now open warfare with Putin's tanks and rockets destroying huge tracts of the cities they have invaded. Many of the citizens of Ukraine have had to leave their homes, hospitals have been destroyed and the homeless have fled to other countries. Putin previously said that it was not his intention to invade Ukraine, as he has, so his word cannot be taken as being binding. Ukraine is being supported by many outlying countries, including Australia.

The world is holding its breath and wondering how China will react if Putin is successful. Why Russia is behaving as it has is a mystery. What are Putin's long term ambitions? The western world appears to be in a quandary. How sane is Putin, how balanced and is he healthy, both physically and mentally healthy? He has a reputation for having his critics murdered.

Would he unleash a nuclear holocaust? Are his longer term aims compatible with the desires of the rest of the world, including China? There have been several of Putin's critics murdered or poisoned.

It does not appear that there is any doubt that Putin wields extreme power and is quite prepared to use that power ruthlessly. There are also reports that, even though he professes to lead a spartan life, he has accumulated huge wealth and property with a value of $285 billion. It is a concern that a person with his power has turned to building his own wealth and position and consorting with "oligarchs," instead of using his talents to foster development and peace in Russia and its satellite countries and, eventually, world peace. He is not a man of peaceful development.

- *Donald Trump.* Trump was selected as its candidate for Presidency of the USA by the Republican Party for the election in 2016, despite the facts that he had been a member of the Democratic Party, the Reform Party, and the Republican Party, twice, previously. In the presidential election he defeated Hilary Clinton by a narrow margin. I found it strange that the USA could not find better and less militant candidates to lead it than a billionaire TV star who had been bankrupted several times, and the wife of a past president of doubtful morality, who had accepted his failings.

I still find it strange that what has been the most successful country of the modern age (until China arose) could not find more thoughtful, better balanced, more moral, and less militant leaders – leaders whose aims are peace and raising the standards of living of the human race – than this pair. Trump is a complicated man, and he is a fighter, not a peacemaker. He has been accused of being a racist and a misogynist based on statements he has made. He does not consider the widely held view of the scientific community that the production of CO_2 is causing climate change and that, therefore, its production must be controlled, to be correct. He slashed the budget for renewable energy research.

Trump's foreign policy was one of "America first" but his actions do not appear to have been cohesive. As President he made decisions with which members of his party, the Republican Party, did not agree. For instance, he withdrew American troops from Syria in October 2019, a decision that was voted against by the US House of Representatives by the surprising margin of 354 to 60.

What the disparate world needs now is leaders whose aims are mutual development, the clearing out of the ridiculous stockpiles of arms – especially nuclear arms – and whose aim is to achieve peace for all. Trump is not such a person. He is a competitor who will go to any length to win. He is not a person whose aims are peaceful settlements.

Trump was defeated in his attempt at a second term as President, meaning that over half of the electors who voted decided that Joseph R. Biden's were safer hands. Whether or not this is an improvement is open to doubt. Biden has supported every war the USA has started in his 47-year political career, and he continues to support American aggression despite promising a more civilised America. Where the USA goes Australia will be obliged to follow.

My list is not comprehensive, and it has an interesting feature. There are no peacemakers in it and no female leaders because I could think of only two female peacemakers from the past who qualified – Mother Teresa and Florence Nightingale. Angela Merkel, Golda Meir, Indira Gandhi, Margaret Thatcher and Theresa May were the only recent, international female political leaders I came up with. Why are leaders who are aiming at advancing civilisation peacefully not represented? Why does the bulk of humanity follow war mongers, not leaders who strive for peace, respect for all, and mutual prosperity?

Given past history, and the present leaderships of the more powerful countries of the world, is there any possibility of humanity overcoming its dangerous squabbles and uniting to lead peaceful and productive existences – or will the weaknesses of the human psyche lead to destruction and possibly annihilation – destruction that will benefit no-one?

Will the ever-increasing population of humans grow to a stage at which it exceeds the production capacity of the globe on which we live and lead to people dying or living in miserable circumstances, as so many Africans and Indians now do? Or will humanity realise that uncontrolled breeding is destructive, and that the population must be limited to a certain number to avoid exceeding the continuous production capacity of our limited globe?

In my view it is now time for humanity to realise its dangers and to change from being a motley collection of squabbling, naked apes of different colours and features, of different beliefs about afterlife, and of different man-made religions, to being a controlled, peaceful, united group of disparate parts in which each has the aims of leading productive and fulfilling lives and who do not want to overload our Earth, our one and only home. Is this possible or is humanity so compounded that it cannot live peacefully and productively?

There are roadblocks to universal peace. The major powers of the world are all arming for "defence" and delight in showing off their armed might. The arms industries of the USA and other leading countries are financially and politically powerful groups, and they will certainly resist being dismantled. Is there any way that the disparate parts of humanity can be brought together and led to agree to abandon their destructive arms in such a way that they will all willingly comply? Unless this can be peacefully accomplished there is little hope for peace – and I doubt that it can be accomplished given the nature of so many of the humans involved and the population of the USA, the western world's leading nation, being wedded to its guns.

It is a possibility that early education, which teaches that each individual must strive to benefit their society, could be the starting point for a better world. Such balanced education could give us the opportunity to live harmoniously. The alternative appears to be that one of the more aggressive religions, or racial groups, will gain the upper hand and dictate to the rest of the world's population how they are to live and worship.

It is a possibility that early education, which teaches that each individual must strive to benefit their society, could be the starting point for a better world. Such balanced education could give us the opportunity to live harmoniously. The alternative appears to be that one of the more aggressive religions, or racial groups, will gain the upper hand and dictate to the rest of the world's population how they are to live and worship.

It appears to me that humanity must now make up its mind as to how it will conduct itself in the future. It can repeat the stupidities of the past and proceed to have conflicts that will benefit no-one except the makers of weapons (and that group only temporarily), or it can put down its weapons, work at raising the standards of living of all humans, attempt to save our globe from pollution, agree to educate the young in a balanced manner that stresses the necessity for each to support their Community peacefully, and work together to unravel the mysteries of our Earth and the Universe.

To succeed in this, humanity requires leaders with characters that are different to those currently in charge. Leaders need to have the following characteristics;

- Their aims must be the peaceful cooperation of all branches of humanity. Unless this can be achieved, and if the various religious, ethnic and cultural groups cannot agree to such cooperation, humanity is unlikely to have a peaceful and productive future.

- They need to have an intelligent understanding of history and of the forces that have caused previous destructive wars, and they need to be able to counter those forces.
- Their driving force must be treating all parts of the disparate racial groups, religions and cultural groups, equally and reasonably, not domination by the group to which they belong. The cycle of a country rising to a controlling eminence by force and subduing other countries, then fading – as discussed by Ray Dalio in his book *"The Changing World Order"* – must be abandoned. Civilisation must change. Its leaders must have a driving force to better all peoples, or societies will destroy themselves..
- They need to encourage, and make available, early basic and balanced education of the young by balanced, educated and unbiased teachers.

If such leaders can be found, and will accept the challenges of leading, humanity can thrive. If humanity continues to have militant, rocket waving dictators and "toughs" leading it, the future looks bleak. As I originally edited this manuscript, I heard that Ukraine was preparing to defend itself against Russia, which had massed troops on Ukraine's boarder while the rest of the world held its breath and hoped for a peaceful outcome. Instead, Russia invaded and started destroying buildings and killing people. What does Putin expect to get from his invasion except dead bodies and ruins? What drives a leader to such a ridiculous extreme? Is he sane? Will the Ukraine ever recover? Will Russia, in time, regret having a neighbour whose citizens hate it? Putin might want to rebuild the USSR but taking an unwilling country by force is no way to achieve peaceful unification.

It is now time for our leaders to call a halt to threatening bickering and displays of destructive weaponry and to try to determine how peace and development can be achieved for the benefit of humanity. For this, necessary, set of actions to take place requires a different set of leaders from those now in charge. As I have already written, we need persons of peace, intelligence, an understanding of history and a regard for all parts of the human race, in charge.

The difficult questions are – will humanity unite and agree to follow intelligent and peaceful leaders of character, balanced education and with the best interests of humanity at heart, and will those with the necessary leadership qualifications accept the positions of leadership? Why would people of talent and energy, those with leadership qualities, want to join the political systems as they now operate, in the adversarial maelstroms that are today's western democracies, and the systems now in charge in Russia and China, when they can use their talents to carve themselves financial niches in the commercial world, succeed in the world of knowledge and the fields of construction and manufacturing, the important area of food production and even in the entertainment field?

I am afraid that given Australia's politicians' penchants for verbal brawling, for bullying, for denigrating their opposite numbers, and for generally attempting one-up-man-ship, people with the talents necessary to provide successful leadership will not want to become involved in the political world.

That world will largely be left to combatants as it is now – unionists with their limited aim of obtaining the best financial result for their members, lawyers trained in an adversarial system, aggressive persons, and self-seekers whose aim is wielding power for self-satisfaction or for the opportunity to accumulate wealth. That is not to say that today all members of parliaments are aggressive self-seekers but, based on their track records even those entering politics with the aim of providing balanced leadership can succumb to the lure of wielding power and the accumulation of money. How did Bob Hawke accumulate his reported $20 million plus fortune?

So, the overriding questions are – how do the world's governments get the politicians and leaders they need given the flaws in the present system, and are there systems that get people with the necessary talents and motivations into leadership roles? Is there a democratic system that appears to work?

The peaceful country of Switzerland might provide a template with its system, which has been described as a direct democracy. What follows is a brief resume of that system.

It has three levels of government that share power and represent the confederation. These are the federal government, the representatives of the 26 cantons, and the local representatives of the 2250 communities, who are elected.

The executive level of government is known as the Federal Council (The Bundesrat). It holds executive power and is made up of seven members who are selected from the next level down, the Federal Assembly, every four years, based on the parties that have the highest shares of the popular vote. The Federal Councillors rotate and each year the role of President is taken by a new nominee. To be a Councillor, or even the President, is thus a period of service, not a sinecure, although it is possible to be the President more than once – but not in consecutive years.

The Swiss parliament is known as the Federal Assembly. It has 246 members who are elected by the eligible voters. There are two levels to the Federal Assembly. The Council of the States (known as the upper chamber) has 46 members, and the National Council (the lower chamber) has 200 members. Members serve on a part time basis. This bicameral arrangement is voted on by eligible voters who are older than 18 years and who follow one of the 15 political parties that exist. Of the population of 8.2 million those able to vote number some 5.3 million.

Each of the 26 cantons has sovereignty and agreement that their sovereignty is not limited by federal law except for such things as weights and measures, civil and criminal law and other matters that require uniformity for the country to operate properly. The cantons operate separately, with each having its own set of laws and its own constitution based on the general rules laid down by the Federal Assembly.

Then there is the Swiss judiciary. There are two branches to the judiciary. The first is the federal judiciary that consists of the Federal

Supreme Court, the Federal Criminal Court, the Federal Patent Court, and the Federal Administration Court. Each canton also has its own courts that hear cases, at first instance, that fall into their jurisdiction. Judges are selected by the parliament or the people.

The final branch of this complex system is that laws can be the subjects of referendums. The Swiss democratic system is unique among western democratic nations in that the system practices direct democracy in parallel with the representative democracy described earlier in this essay. Swiss referendums are direct votes by eligible citizens on proposals that can have national, cantonal, or local consequences. More than 550 referendums have been held since the constitution of 1848 was formed.

Switzerland has managed to remain neutral during Europe's more recent World Wars. It has also managed to remain prosperous (its GDP per head is the highest in the world except for the small state of Luxembourg), despite it having little in the way of natural resources except mountainous scenery and lakes. The Swiss are industrious. I believe that Australia can learn from Switzerland.

I recognise that to change the Australian political system will be a massive task and that many, especially those who are gaining financially from the existing system, will object, but I consider that this important matter should be considered. A select group could be commissioned to prepare a new constitution that is then presented to the voting population of Australia for ratification or dismissal.

I also consider that the future of humanity, as a whole, is probably the most important matter that is now facing our world. It should be central to the thinking of our best intelligences. We must stop the ridiculous arms race, provide balanced education for the young, investigate the sustainable population of our Earth, cease the wars between tribes, countries, races and religions, and change humanity's attitudes from the existing stupidity of arming for peace to one of cooperating for future successes.

Will we manage to work together for a peaceful Earth, or will we continue to slowly overload and poison our home? Will groups of us continue to arm themselves for "peace", the inevitable outcome of which will be war?

Already, as I write this in April 2022, Russian forces have invaded Ukraine and are shelling buildings and killing ordinary citizens. Refugees are being forced to leave their homes during winter. The army of Ukraine, aided by help from interested countries, is fighting a gallant battle but their buildings are being destroyed. From this war there will be no victors – only destruction. It is a human tragedy.

Why Vladimir Putin has set these wheels of war in motion is not clear to me. He appears to want a more powerful and productive Russia under his command, but it is unlikely that he will achieve this aim by ruining Ukraine.

He is probably concerned and feels threatened by being surrounded by NATO forces and is striking early. What he hopes to gain from ruining a country, that he hopes to unite with his own, is also unclear. Perhaps it is Ukraine's productive capacities, especially its food producing farms, that he hopes to control. Its production of seed crops (barley, maize, wheat and sunflower seeds), meat (chicken, pork beef and veal), and other primary food products such as potatoes and sugar beet might explain Putin's aim – to have the Ukraine as a food supplier for greater Russia.

His excuse for his armed attack is that Ukraine wants to join NATO, which would put a potential enemy and armaments on his doorstep. The western world, including Australia, considers this a feeble excuse for Putin's invasion but that same western world is objecting to China establishing a base on the Solomon Islands, some 2000km from Australia because it could be a threat to our safety.

Before universal peace can be attained the western allies have the immediate problem of how to handle the Ukraine mess. The western allies are afraid of getting too heavy handed with the defence of Ukraine because it could lead a desperate Putin to use his nuclear arsenal. Unless Putin can be persuaded to adopt a more statesmanlike approach there cannot be anything but a sad ending to this mess.

It is time to put down weapons of destruction and to move on from the stupidities of wars, to disarm and to educate the young that solving the challenges of peace are much more satisfying than being involved in the ravages of conflict.

2. HUMANITY'S RISES, FALLS, AND FUTURE POSSIBILITIES.

Once, not so long ago, it was part of the instruction of the educated young that they had duties to their family and their society. A private school even still has as its motto "Duty". Duty meant an obligation to fulfill legal and moral responsibilities. Today the word is hardly ever used to imply responsibility for practical, legal, or moral matters. It is usually reserved for the armed forces and for those engaged in attempting to protect society from law breakers.

Why? Why is it not generally taught to the young, in western societies, that they have a moral duty to their society to live in a positive and productive manner? A society that lives by a tenet of contribution by its citizens is a society that is growing more creative and healthy. A society in which many of its citizens believe they are entitled to be provided for by the government and vote themselves benefits from the public purse is a society in moral and financial decline.

The history of societies shows that in the past civilisations have gone from periods of barbarism through periods of energetic development, to periods of decadence as their energies weakened. Where, on this cycle, is the current western world and where is China? Where is the USA and where is Australia?

An example is the Greek civilisation that started in the 8th century BCE and fell to the Romans in 146BC. Their Hellenistic culture has affected western societies ever since. Today Greece is no longer a leading power.

In the western world Greece was followed by Rome, which is reputed to have been founded by Romulus in 753BC, and spread out from that city, taking control of much of southern Europe and the Mediterranean coast of Africa. Rome even invaded and brought civilisation to southern England and built roads, viaducts, aqueducts, and impressive buildings throughout its energetic empire. Despite its successes the Roman empire was never a settled or stable empire. There were continuous conflicts by those seeking power and position. Eventually the empire broke into two parts and the western part, which was subject to internal warring, was attacked and conquered by the Goths led by Alaric (370 – 410 AD). Rome's heyday was over.

Since Rome was defeated other power groups have arisen and continue to do so to this day. The religions, both the Christian religion and the Muslim religion, had periods of being in power, with the Muslim religion taking over much of southern Europe and northern Africa until 1492 and the Christian religion making unsuccessful crusades between 1095 and 1303. How anybody can regard Christianity as the creation of a benevolent and peaceful God given its history and its treatment of non-Christians is a mystery. And the Muslim religion also has a terrible track record, with its murdering of thousands in its attack on the World Trade Centre in New York, in 2001, being just one recent, notable crime.

Humanity continues to follow its several different religions despite their inhuman track records. Empires continue to be created and to fail in time as they lose their energies. The cycles of empires rising on a tide of energy and ability from their citizens, as the Romans did, as the British Empire did, as the USA is now entering into the final stages of doing, and as China is in the earlier stages of doing, and of then losing their drives and slowly deteriorating, is still happening. Surely it is time to end these stupid and destructive cycles of growth, deterioration and conflict, and for humanity to unite to find the most balanced and beneficial way forward for all.

The fastest rising, most energetically driven modern power is China. It has a long and mixed history of conflicts and productive periods that ended with the Qing dynasty, (1644 – 1912) when a new power arose – the People's Republic of China (PRC).

The British and the French had previously subdued the Chinese in the Opium Wars, the second of which took place from 1856 to 1860. This is a disgraceful period of British history. China remained a backward country until 1912 when the PRC was formed after a revolution, led by Sun Yat-sen, was successful. Civil wars ensued for decades. In 1949 the PRC, based on communism and led by Mao Zedong, became the ruling government. Following Mao's access to power came what is now known as "The Great Leap Forward" during which millions died. Since Mao's death there have been several power struggles that have resulted in China transitioning from a planned economy to what has been a success – a mixed economy known as "Market Socialism". Under this system, and fueled by an energetic population anxious to learn and contribute, China has boomed. It is a hive of activity at all levels. Now its leader, Xi Jinping, appears to be attempting to revert to a more hard line communist governing approach. Billionaires beware.

China is now the most financially powerful country on planet Earth. For the future welfare of humanity it has a duty to use its power for the benefit of the planet – but will it meet that duty, or will it wield its power to lash those societies who have treated it so appallingly in the past? What China has accomplished to date is remarkable, even awe inspiring. What it does from here on will affect the rest of humanity greatly.

As the USA loses its position as the world's most powerful nation, and as its energy levels fall as the expectation levels of its citizens rise, and their performance levels deteriorate, China will grow in importance and power. For a period, China could then dictate how the world operates. It is already showing dictatorial signs in its dealings with lesser countries such as Australia. Once it has established itself as the pre-eminent power it will probably slowly slide into a period of self-satisfaction and will lose its pre-eminence, and is likely to repeat the history of earlier leading countries that have withered. Where will the next leading power arise? Africa? Russia? India? Or will humanity mature, realise that we can unite and all enjoy better living standards, and that we can all can live in peace?

Of course, the rise and fall of a dominant group could all be changed by a nuclear conflict, or by balanced education that clearly shows the faults of the past, as empires have risen and fallen. If humanity can be shown that our weapons are now so destructive that wars are no longer battles for superiority, but are paths to extinction and huge destruction, as the current battles in Ukraine, that are really minor battles, are showing, and that heterogeneous humanity has no alternative but to live together peacefully and develop systems that are beneficial to all groups, not just the group who happens to be the elite of that period. I hope that humanity has the intelligence and the moral courage to meet this challenge, to give up its ridiculous tribal/religious/ethnic and destructive wrangling, and to realise that we must all win together, or we will all lose. The alternative to all winning is gross destruction. Samples of such destruction are already under way in Ukraine and Syria. Unfortunately, I do not have a great deal of faith in the human race to see what, to me, is so clear.

The first steps are that we give up our ethnic, our political and our religious wrangles, we stop arming for conflict, and we educate the young in a balanced manner, so that they learn they have duties to humanity and its societies. The young must be told that each has a duty to produce useful artefacts, thoughts, cures for diseases, nourishing foods and, most importantly, that they must educate their young in a balanced way.

Those who are the leaders of our societies are currently those who seek political power and/or those who seek wealth. These are not likely to be the best drivers of our societies. Humanity needs leaders whose aims are the betterment of all humanity. The Putins of the world with their lust for power and position are destructive and those who seek to accumulate wealth to attract notoriety are unlikely to be the leaders humanity needs.

Contributing to society is not a path to a glorious life after death, it is a necessity for the welfare and continued existence of humanity in the future, and is its own reward. Creation, construction and production must surely be more satisfying aims for balanced people than destruction.

3. THE IMPORTANCE OF US.

There are two questions I have often asked myself – how important in the total scheme of things, in our vast universe, are we humans, and are we as important as many of us consider we are – so important that each of us has an all-powerful deity watching over us? My personal answers to each of these questions is "no". We are not as important as many in the Christian and Moslem worlds have made themselves out to be, with their ridiculous belief that we are made in the likeness of a supreme being and that by worshipping their God each individual will be granted everlasting life in paradise.

This wishful thinking does not stand scrutiny in my opinion. Where are the lines drawn? Do Neanderthals and the other early humanoids get to heaven? If not, why not? What has happened to all of the "natives" who have lived and died – the red Indians, the early oriental groups of Asia, the Australian aborigines, and the many tribes of Africa and South America – who for tens of thousands of years lived and died without having heard of Christ or Allah?

Surely an all-knowing, all-loving deity would not allow the gift of heaven to be given to only those born less than 2000 years ago (or in the case of Moslems some 1400 years ago)? What is so special about squabbling humans that only they have been selected to enjoy an everlasting happy life after death?

Humanity's only claim to supremacy is that we are probably the most intelligent of the Earth's creatures. We understand some complex matters, we can make complicated things – such as machines and chemical compounds and we can communicate quite complicated ideas to each other. On the downside, a big percentage of humans are still currently quarrelsomely tribal, have unproven beliefs they are ready to kill and to die for, and can be thoroughly self-centred.

Given the vastness of space, the innumerable galaxies and other suns that fill it, and with the possibilities of those suns having planets with conditions that could support life forms, it is more than possible that other life forms do exist out in space – it is likely.

Since humanity became sentient and able to consider abstract matters, it has searched for answers as to why it, and its supporting animals and vegetation, exist, how living things came into being, and what can be done to prolong limited life spans. Once humanity changed from being nomadic hunter gatherers to being agrarian – although not all tribes achieved that leap prior to the development of sailing ships – it started to consider difficult questions. Questions such as why are we here? Is there a purpose to humanity's life on Earth or are we just another unimportant life form? Are there supreme intelligences watching how each of us performs? Is there life after death and if there is how can each of us achieve it? There are many answers to those, and other, questions but there is no proof that any of the large number of religions that humanity has put together are anything other than paths to importance for their leaders, or the result of imaginings of single persons with virtually no proofs that their tenets are real.

Hundreds of religions have been formulated, many have beliefs that are similar, and many have been formed by peoples with no access to other religions, so they are not copies but arose out of original thoughts. Most, especially the earlier religions, were polytheistic. Today the leading religions are Christianity, Islam, Hinduism, and

Buddhism. Judaism has a much smaller following in numbers, but it is disproportionately powerful, and atheism and agnosticism are growing.

The facts that most of the religions that were once so powerful have faded into obscurity (examples are the Greek and Roman Gods and the Gods of Egypt) and that several of the more prominent religions are losing believers at present, indicate that the beliefs of the world could be changing. On the evidence that many of the ancient religions have been abandoned and that large areas of the world now do not follow any orthodox religion, it is probable that religions, as we know them, will slowly disappear as balanced education gets through to more of the young populations and we learn more about humanity and its existence.

However, a large percentage of the world's population needs a guiding hand it can trust. So it is unlikely that religions, which came into being out of a psychological need in the populations of the world to have such a guiding hand, will disappear. What I hope is that religions that survive will all agree to behave peacefully, and that religions that are currently prepared to enlarge their numbers by quelling and conquering will change to being peaceful so that humanity will thrive. I also hope that religions that encourage large families, to increase the numbers of their adherents, also recognise that there is a limit to the number of people our Earth can sustain, and encourage population control. It is possible that homosexuality is not the sin it is made out to be by some religions, but is nature's way of helping control population growth.

Having put forward arguments for doing away with religions on the grounds that they are not divinely inspired but are the constructs of humans, I also consider that if they had not been desired by humanity they would not have grown as they have, and they would not have become as important as they are. So to help bolster the self-importance of that part of humanity that needs it, perhaps we should retain religions so that those who wish to can be part of their chosen religion. They can then receive the comfort of looking forward to a secure life after death – a life of peace, satisfaction, and fulfilment in a warm and enjoyable heaven. Current religions will then either thrive and attract adherents or will wither away as better education spreads or alternatives religions arise, as they have in the past.

Because we humans are, almost certainly, the most intelligent of the living things on our Earth, we have inherited the role of protector of the environment. This does not mean that our only responsibility is to look after the long-term well-being of humanity. It also means that we have the responsibility of making sure that there are environments that are suitable for other living creatures and plants. We must try not to make our planet unsuitable for other living things. Surely the first step to achieving a world that is balanced and that can support its living creatures and plants is to limit humanity's numbers to a sustainable level. Just what that number is has not yet been ascertained, but it is quite possible that it has already been passed and that we are already poisoning our home. We need to find what the number of humans is for balance, and we need to persuade those who, traditionally, have large families that, for humanity's sake, they must limit the number of their children. If we cannot meet these challenges we will, eventually, destroy our support system. Humanity must realise that it must not overwhelm nature or we will poison our Earth.

In the great scheme of things, we humans, and our current animal and vegetable co-habitants, that are our life supports, on our tiny planet Earth, in the vastness of space, are unimportant. We should recognise that and act accordingly. We should present a united face to the challenges that will, inevitably, beset us – new and more virulent diseases, climate changes that we cannot control, the cluttering of our planet with our debris, and the increasing population with its requirement for sustenance and medical support. It is quite idiotic that humanity has not recognised that we need our best intelligences solving these problems as they arise and that we, instead, arm ourselves and kill each other.

Many mysteries of our small patch of space remain to be solved. Let us accept that we present and future humans are no more important than the Neanderthals were, and put our energies into the task of deciphering the wonders of our universe, not into murdering each other.

4. GIVING OR TAKING?

In Australia today, newspapers, magazines and television screens are awash with demands by "special" groups who expect benefits from the public purse for their well-being. These groups are supported in their demands by candidates for office, and parliamentary parties, who make promises to provide facilities, equipment, accommodation, health controls and living expenses that are to a standard that is higher than many other countries can afford.

This buying of votes drains the public purse and leads to our parliaments containing people who, in many instances, are not those who should be leading the country.

We need leaders who are experienced, who have an understanding of the commercial world, who look to the future and to improving living and working conditions for all humans – not those who are seeking important positions and a public profile. Parliaments are not places for self-seekers. They should be places for caring and knowledgeable citizens who wish to serve their society and future generations. We need people who are prepared to give a period of their lives to improving their country's living and working conditions for all.

Does our Westminster System, as practised in Australia, meet these requirements? Are western democracies slowly and noticeably crumbling financially in a welter of welfare expenditure for votes?

The demand for benefits from the public purse is understandable in some ways, but it is a pathway to the deterioration of western democracies. That demand is fueled by the fact that our democratic system provides opportunities for some to accumulate extreme levels of wealth and, having acquired it they then allow magazines to advertise that wealth, often unearned, having been passed down from a previous successful generation. These displays of wealth can lead average voters to believe that they too are entitled to a share of this wealth bounty.

We, lucky citizens of Australia, with our saleable coal, iron ore and gas, and our production of foods, are having a fairly easy ride to prosperity – but should it continue, and will it continue, given the current concern about the dangers of global warming from higher levels of CO_2 in our atmosphere? Will China continue to pay high prices for our coal and iron ore when those prices are considerably higher than the cost of production? Why is China prepared to pay these prices? Is it because the bulk of the profit from the sales is returned to China? Does China have a long-term strategy that we do not understand, or is China a major shareholder of the mining companies (and other western companies) and, therefore, the secret recipient of a major part of the profits? These questions need to be asked and answered. How much of the Fortescue Metals Group does China actually own? Why is FMG's ownership not widely known?

Because there are so many rich in Australia and because their wealth is so blatantly advertised, the general population is led into believing that their share of the wealth of their country should be greater. They do not consider that we are living in a competitive world and that the general level of wealth is dependent on the general levels of effort and efficiency when compared with those levels in other countries.

There are groups of people in Australia who appear to believe that because of their ethnicity, even a partial ethnicity, and the unfortunate histories of their forebears, they are entitled to special moral and financial treatments regardless of their personal contributions to their mixed society. These Australians, who contribute little or nothing to their general society, consider that they are entitled to a share of Australia's wealth, wealth that has been created by others, purely because of their ethnicity. I disagree with this attitude. It is my belief that everyone should try to energetically contribute to their society, both because it creates a healthier and wealthier Australia, and because it provides those contributing with a sense of purpose and the satisfaction of accomplishment. No one should be able to take from their society without contributing because they were born into a particular race or into a particular family.

Then there are those who suffer from age, chronic illness, and mental problems. Society has a duty to care for these. Those who do the caring are contributing to the overall wellbeing of their society and are to be commended.

It is my view that each citizen of Australia has a duty to contribute to the welfare of our country to the best of their individual capabilities. No one should take pride in being a mendicant and no one should accept largesse from their government and fritter it away wastefully – especially on drugs. There is a pride in producing more than is consumed. Those accepting benefits from the public purse who are not contributing as best they can, do not get to experience that pride.

Many Australians appear to believe that they are important simply because they are alive. This is not so. For a human being to be important it is necessary for that human to contribute to their society to the best of their ability. To live a life of taking and not producing or caring for those less fortunate, or a life of stealing, selling illicit drugs or vandalising, is unsatisfying and unsatisfactory. Such a life leads to moral deterioration.

At this time in the democratic western world too many politicians are attempting to be voted into positions of political power by promising to distribute their country's wealth, even wealth that is not yet earned, to voters so that those voters will cast votes for them. Is it reasonable that a vote from an indigent taker is as valuable as a vote from a worthwhile contributor? Is there a morally reasonable alternative? Although I see the weakness in the present system I do not think there is a fairer alternative. Whether or not a citizen becomes a mendicant, a thief or a dealer of drugs can depend, to a degree, on a person's upbringing, their education and their inherent nature, but it remains a matter of personal choice.

Unless those who vote with the aim of increasing their take, change their attitudes, and vote for candidates who have as their aim a long term prosperous and vital Australia, there will continue to be a breakdown of our country's moral fibre and a deterioration of our performance on the world stage. The tough, able, self-sacrificing and independent Aussie battlers, so well thought of during two World Wars, now exists only in pockets – and these are decreasing.

What Australia, and the rest of the western democratic world, needs is a resurgence of what used to be called the Anzac spirit. More attention must be given to what contribution each of us can make to our society, and less emphasis must be given to what our society can do for each individual. Each of us must realise that only by carrying out our duties as well, and as efficiently, as we can and not demanding excessive monetary rewards can Australia compete in world markets.

All Australians recognise that to win sporting contests – cricket, polo, golf, football, athletics, swimming, and team sports of all descriptions – those competing must have natural abilities and must devote their time and energies to refining those abilities, do so, and appear to gain satisfaction from doing so. That spirit of working towards success in sports is applauded, and stars who are successful become rich and are given public awards.

However, people who devote their lives to productive, educational and health controlling pursuits – people who grow our food, build, and maintain our necessary infrastructure, those who spend their lives educating the young and those who tend the damaged of our society – certainly do not get the attention that sports stars get. Why? Are the producers, educators and those tending our health not as worthy of attention and accolade as someone who can throw a large ball through a netted hoop?

Then there are the wasters and vandals of our societies who make claims on the government, who steal from their fellow citizens, and who destroy the properties and vehicles of those who have worked to own those assets. They are a blot on the society in which they live. It is hard for me to believe that they find satisfaction in their destructive lifestyles. I believe that moral parenting and balanced early education – early parenting and education which teaches that serving society and that giving, not taking, are their own rewards – would reduce their numbers.

I find it strange that the swankiest buildings in Australia are now casinos. They are not necessarily the best architecturally, but they are impressively showy. They could be taken as a sign that our society is sinking into a period of decadence. While I hope that is not so, I sincerely hope that Australia turns its potential energies away from gambling and into productions that the world wants and can afford. At 90 I am not in a position to help the creative surge that I believe Australia is capable of, but I would certainly like to see such a surge happen before decadence becomes the norm in Australia, as it has for earlier societies.

Unless the givers (the producers, the carers, the educators, the growers, and the infrastructure providers) far outnumber the takers (those who claim government assistance, vandals, thieves, spongers, delinquents, non-producers and even those who demand higher wages than an industry can afford), society falls into a state of sloth and decadence.

Australia is still a young and developing country. I want it to produce and prosper. I want it to achieve its potentials. I do not want to see it spend itself into a swamp of debt as it meets its government's promises to buy votes.

A thriving civilisation is one consisting of more givers than takers. What is Australia's position today and what will it be in the future?

5. WAR AND/OR PEACE 1.

Since Homo sapiens became the most powerful species on our shared planet, Earth, it has conducted itself both admirably – by creating things of technical excellence, of value and of usefulness and beauty – and appallingly – by constantly warring between groups with different skin colours and political and religious beliefs – and by destroying things of beauty and presence, things both natural and things created by other humans.

Humanity has been able to carry out these, incompatible, activities and has still been able to survive because the capabilities of its weapons of war have been limited in their destructive powers.

However, things are changing. It is now my belief that with its ability to develop destructive and contagious diseases, and to harness the powers of atomic fission – both of which can have damaging and long lasting effects – humanity has reached a crossroads. It can continue down the path of further and worse diseases and more destructive weapons, or it can realise that from an all-out conflict there will be no victors – only vicious new diseases, long lasting poisons, mass destruction and, possibly, total oblivion.

Humanity has to now decide whether it wants to live in competitive peace, whether it is willing to be involved in no holds barred conflicts or, possibly, whether it can establish a set of rules to which all powers agree, that will save the world from the complete annihilation of many of its living things

In my view there is really no choice. We must abandon experimenting with contagious diseases. We must also stop the flashy shows of weapons of destruction and machines of war, we must stop producing them, and we must abandon those we already have. Most importantly we must agree to abandon nuclear weapons.

We must also persuade the many militants among us, especially those that believe in the superiority of their race or religion and that condone the killing of those not of those races or religions, that the only way humanity can thrive is for it to put the greater part of human effort into a better, fairer and more equitable world.

We must attempt to live peacefully together and to help each other. Unfortunately, human nature being what it has been so far, I am not optimistic about the various warring parties putting down their arms and competing peacefully on production. As I see it, it is a case of we all win or we all lose.

6. WAR AND/OR PEACE 2.

Countries, religions and ethnic groups that make up the Earth's human population – Orientals, Europeans, Arabs, Indians, Slavs, the various races of Africa, North and South America and the Pacific and Indian Ocean islands, and the small but important and independent groups such as the Israelis, the Eskimos, the Nepalese and the offspring of the original inhabitants of Australia – have not yet learnt to live peacefully together. Many are fighting battles or are preparing their "defences" for war.

Why? Humanity only has one Earth so we should be peacefully deciding how to share it for the most benefit of all, and attempting to ascertain the total population that can be supported in a balanced manner. We should be concentrating on how we can live together peacefully and share our finite and limited world. Instead we, as mixed races, spend our time, mental efforts and huge sums of money on tools of war for "defence". To achieve peaceful agreements requires that the disparate groups behave in a balanced and honourable manner. Is this likely to happen?

Currently many countries, including Australia, are spending a good deal of human intelligence and large sums of money on training warriors, advanced weaponry and war machines – warships, submarines, land vehicles, sophisticated fighting aircraft and destructive missiles – all in the name of "defence". Humanity's efforts, and money, should not be spent on weapons of war but on achieving peaceful agreements. If everyone is armed for "defence" sooner or later someone will hit the wrong button and the world could go up in flames. Training warriors to kill other people and equipping them with sophisticated weapons to accomplish that task is not what civilised humanity should be doing in this day and age.

Is training for war a sensible activity in today's world? Is it possible for the various parts of humanity with their differences and their different beliefs to realise that we only have one globe on which to live, and that war will despoil much of our home and will result in the ruination of some of our prized treasures?

If the time, mental effort and money used to create the many weapons of "defence" were put into producing food more efficiently, and to producing such things as comfortable modes of travel for we humans to enjoy, surely the world would be a better place for both humanity and its supporting animals. Or are we humans so made that we must continue with our ridiculous, expensive and destructive conflicts?

As I write this it is now mid-October 2021. Afghanistan is in the hands of fundamentalist Moslem males who are denying women equal rights. In other parts of the world the leadership of nations is controlled by militant males who appear, by their actions, to be aiming at leaving their names in history alongside those of Stalin, Adolph Hitler and Mao Zedong all of whom presided over the deaths of millions of their subjects and their enemies.

It is probably self-evident that there is little hope of populations changing from preparing for war, using as their excuse that they are preparing their defences, when the leaders are such people as Vladimir Putin, Joe Biden, Kim Jon-un and, especially, Xi Jinping who appears to be harbouring a deep seated resentment of the western world. He could be still smarting from the manner in which the English and the French treated the Chinese during the Opium Wars in the 19th century.

Given the characters of the leaders there appears to me to be little chance of the world becoming cooperatively peaceful, productive and enjoyable unless there is a change of heart by the leaders and a change of attitude by the countries that follow fundamental Islam.

Why does the human herd follow destructively militant leaders? Why do groups of military minded people, usually mature males, prepare the young for killing and destruction by training them for warfare when the young should be encouraged to contribute to positive endeavours that contribute to the health and well-being of their society.

Then there is the special task, a task that is vital for future peace and prosperity, of educating the young to a balanced curriculum. They should be given guidance into living lives of peaceful and useful endeavours, not lives of willful destruction and death.

China is now heavily armed and is continuing to build its armed might. If it is not for aggression in the future, and possibly war with the western world, why are Xi and his military advisers expending so much of their country's wealth and energy on weapons of destruction and military installations? Xi should be aware that out of armed conflict there will be a winner, but there will not be a glorious victor. There will be many killed and maimed and many of the worthwhile creations of humanity will be destroyed. The question that intrigues me is – what are Xi's long term aims? I am sure he has them.

Although I have no idea of what the long term aims of Xi and his military advisers are I suspect that they are not peaceful. I also cannot understand why China is seeking military might when it is peacefully taking over so much of our planet's construction, fabrication, and manufacturing markets anyway.

Finally, I do not understand why China is being so heavy handed with Taiwan. To risk a nuclear holocaust to gain sovereignty over a country that does not want to be part of China and will remain a thorn in China's side if it is taken over, seems foolish – and I do not believe the leadership of China is foolish. China's energy levels have been impressive, and its development has been spectacular.

Then there are the other major armed powers, the chief of which is the U. S of A. Since World War 2 it has been the most powerful and best armed country on planet Earth, a position it will not willingly relinquish. Now it is being challenged by a fast developing China. Unless both China and America realise they are on a path to armed conflict and that out of that conflict there will be no winner, only death and damage to many and destruction of many of humanity's better creations – supply systems of essentials such as clean water, food and electrical power, communications systems, transport systems, hospitals with their miracle facilities, systems and medicines, and the many infrastructures that service our modern world. Why would thoughtful humanity risk destruction of these creations in wars that will produce wreckage and poison areas of conflict but will gain nothing for the survivors except the knowledge that they were the winners and that they have control of the mess that has been created. Surely no-one can see value in such mass destruction.

The leaders of China, and most other countries, must realise that for humanity to advance in the future the following activities are necessary:

- The young must be educated in a balanced and factual manner, without bias, on the history of humanity, its successes and its failures, its virtues and its vices. The young need to understand why the stupidities of the past – the mass deaths and destructions – have taken place so that such stupidities are not repeated in the future. There must be no further brain washing of the young by militant and aggressive leaders or religious bigots seeking access to power and position.
- There must be no further judging of a person's worth by the colour of that person's skin. All races must be treated similarly. A corollary to that requirement is that no racial group should be entitled to special privileges just because they are of an ethnic group. All must be expected to contribute to their society to the extent of their abilities.
- There must be no discrimination based on the sex, or the sexual

proclivities, of any person. Males and females, heterosexuals and homosexuals must be treated equally. Of course, all sexual activity must remain as being by mutual consent. If there is unforced agreement, what is being done in private is not an offence, in my view. There must still be no coercion involved and minors must still be protected from predators.

- Discrimination on the basis of a person's religious beliefs is not to be supported but, in return, religions must not attempt to coerce susceptible people into accepting unproven beliefs.
- My own view is that none of the religions are based on the word of an almighty God, and that the history of the disagreements and wars between religions, and the destruction that is done by religious fanatics to the present day, indicates that some religions are not peaceful or supportive of humanity. However as so many people find comfort in peaceful religions they can be accepted – but they cannot behave aggressively as they have in the past and as sects of the Moslem religion are still doing today.
- Humanity has now accumulated so much knowledge that it is not possible for one mind to encompass it all. However it is important that the basic 3R's (reading, writing and arithmetic) are taught and that education is balanced. The most important lesson is that each of us has the responsibility of serving our society as best we can so that societies prosper. A healthy and prosperous society, one in which each individual attempts to contribute, will provide satisfaction to those who do contribute. There is more to be gained from contributing to society than by taking from it.
- Competition must be friendly and open. Cooperation should be encouraged. Piracy of technology and secret spying should still be a crime but if society develops, as I hope it will, there will be less stealing of ideas and techniques because people will be encouraged to behave honourably.

- It is my hope that a more honourable ethos will develop as humanity realises that behaving honourably benefits not only their society, but also the individuals who behave honourably. There should still be competition and the kudos should be spread to all those competing and not confined to only the winners.

Is there any chance of humanity melding into a united, cooperative group and behaving in a mutually supportive manner, or is it more likely that it will continue with its ridiculous confrontational approaches? It is clear to me that unless we can unite, and make our aims those of mutual respect and mutual support, the likely result will be a destructive holocaust.

Can humanity change from being groups of warring countries, religions and races to being groups that have differences but who have united and peaceful aims? Surely this should be what leaders should be trying to achieve, instead of the current stupidities of leaders flourishing their weapons of destruction, producing large armed forces and adopting war-like postures.

Is there any chance of humanity changing from groups who act as though they are enemies and want to dominate, to being a united front that has the aim of building a better and more balanced world, who takes on the challenges of space and who strives for peace and advancement? Or is humanity doomed by its nature – a nature that was formed in a completely different environment – that will lead it to mass destruction? I can only hope that we will learn to cooperate to our total benefit before we destroy our world.

7. GLOBAL WARMING / CLIMATE CHANGE – A REPRISE.

My 2020 book *"Issues"* contained an essay entitled *"Global Warming – Climate Change."* More recently, in 2021, I was given a copy of a paper entitled *"A Cool Look At Global Warming"* published in 2008 by Professor Don Aitkin, a well credentialed and obviously well-balanced scholar. It has increased my perspective about the vexed question of global warming. This essay is intended to precis both the paper written by Professor Aitkin and my earlier paper because I consider his, considerably longer, paper provides underpinning to my shorter essay and adds weight to it.

In order to provide as full a picture as possible I now summarise the Professor's paper and recommend that any reader who is interested obtains a copy of it because it presents a well balanced view of the situation regarding climate change.

- Professor Aitkin considers that Australia is faced with two major environmental problems, neither of which is global warming. They are – how to manage sufficient water for a dry continent that is moving into a long dry period, and how to find a satisfactory alternative to oil based energy production, as oil is going to run out and is getting more expensive as its supply

Further Issues and Challenges

dwindles. He does not consider that global warming is such an important issue, and he is agnostic about Anthropogenic Global Warming (AGW). I do not know what his basis is for believing that Australia is going to suffer a long dry period.
- In his paper he addresses what is known of the following:
    1. The extent to which the planet is warming.
    2. Whether, or not, such warming is unprecedented.
    3. Whether, or not, the weather is affected by the burning of fossil fuels.
    4. The likelihood of the polar caps melting in a major way.
    5. The accuracy of the computer models that predict future climates.
    6. The reluctance of proponents of global warming to admit uncertainty.
    7. The extent to which we need to change our ways of life to avoid a catastrophe.
- The Professor points out that knowledge is dependent on discovery of scientific facts, and that AGW does not appear to meet the necessary criteria for it to be regarded as a fact. Consensus is not a basis for a theory to be declared a scientific fact.
- He points out that climate science is relatively new and the effects of various factors that create climate – the sun's activities, the oceans, the Earth's magnetic field and its atmosphere, the land masses – are not yet understood clearly enough for scientists to be sure of how climate is affected and to what degree.
- Professor Aitkin is prepared to accept that the Earth is warming, even though there are many doubters. He mentions the Medieval Warm Period (MWP) and the Little Ice Age (LIA). He writes that *"There is nothing especially unprecedented about the 20th century temperature rise"* and quotes a passage from Newsweek dated 28 April 1975 that said a dramatic change in the Earth's weather patterns *"may portend a drastic decline in food production"* and reported that *"Last April"* there had been *"the most devastating outbreak of tornadoes ever recorded."*

- He reported that the small increase in the very small component of CO_2 in the Earth's atmosphere has not been shown to affect climate as is being claimed. He stated that the effect on climate of CO_2 is *"logarithmic and diminishing."* Recent ice core data suggests that temperature change precedes rises in CO_2 levels by about 800 years due to cold seas, which can absorb CO_2, giving up CO_2 as they warm. So the rise in the level of CO_2 in the atmosphere follows the rise in the temperature of the seas. It does not cause warmer conditions.
- He also reported that *"There is no evidence yet that increasing concentrations of CO_2 are harmful to us"* and that *"they certainly increase plant growth vigour."*
- He discusses global warming and its effect on sea levels and reports that there is, as yet no evidence that melting ice will cause catastrophic rises in sea levels.
- He discusses the use of computer modelling of climate. He considers the accuracy of the computer models he has assessed as being unduly reliant on doubtful variables.
- The IPCC reports of 1990, 1995, 2001 and 2007 were accompanied by summaries, the language of which was, in his opinion, more political than scientific. He is also critical of the IPCC's, and the UN's, claims that their reports have the support of thousands of scientists and that there are no dissenters. The IPCC's peer reviews *"do not seem kosher"* to the Professor, who has long term experience in such matters.
- He discusses the tendency of the IPCC scholars to protect their own theories instead of attempting to demolish those propositions. This trend he regards as being the wrong approach. He is also critical of climate change being held to be the cause of unrelated events – *"Fires, storms, trapped polar bears, cold and undue heat."*
- The Professor considers that *"climate change has become a quasi-religious view"* and that there are many, including scientists,

whose livelihood depends on the AGW proposition. He has several other reasons for considering that AGW is not necessarily correct even though it has become the orthodox position.

- He sees no alternative but that humanity accepts that CO_2 will continue to increase in our Earth's atmosphere given that China and India *"will not reduce their own use of carbon."* He wants a fair and open enquiry about AGW with scientists openly discussing the data.
- He states that global warming is a distraction and that the real problems for humanity are water and energy. He urges all those interested to be careful and systematic in finding out what is involved, and to make decisions on climate change *"on the basis of your reading, thinking and discussion."*

The IPCC, the Intergovernmental Panel on Climate Change, has reported that our Earth is warming and that we have only 12 years to prevent a climate change catastrophe by limiting warmings to 1.5 degrees C. The IPCC does not provide a solution as to how the necessary reductions in the production of CO_2, and other greenhouse gases, are to be achieved and how humanity can still provide the electrical power and transport facilities that Earth's inhabitants need.

There is also the fact that the biggest emitters of greenhouse gases are China, India, Russia, the USA and Japan, and that only the USA is cutting down on its production of the gases. Before the western world ruins its economies there must be a more balanced investigation of the situation by independent experts and scientists who have no ties to the, so called, 'renewable' energy producers.

I now summarise my original essay and add some new thoughts.

- I am not surprised that the IPCC has found that our Earth could have major problems with global warming. Had it not found such future problems its researchers would not have reasons for sustaining their important positions. I am also not surprised that there are many who disagree with the IPCC's findings.

If you look at graphs of our Earth's history you will find that the level of CO2 during the early carboniferous period was somewhere between 1500 and 2000 parts per million. The forests of the time absorbed the CO2 so that it fell to very low levels and the oxygen levels rose. The climate changed and the Earth changed markedly. CO2 is still at an historically low levels. There is some doubt that temperatures are rising as the IPCC has predicted. Time will tell who is correct.

- Based on Earth's earlier history its climate has changed dramatically in the distant past. It has even changed quite markedly during the very short period for which humans have kept records. It is almost certain that, given these histories, climate on Earth will continue to change regardless of what we humans do. A belief that what we do to control CO2 will change the climate is certainly undue optimism. What we need to do is prepare for both colder and warmer climates. Both of which call for big and reliable sources of electrical power.

- Today all plant life, and therefore all animal life, depends on the approximately 400 parts per million of CO2 in the Earth's atmosphere. No CO2 – no life.

- In the distant past the Earth has been subjected to periods of frozen conditions and through periods of much higher levels of CO2, which nurtured verdant forests. Climate has never been completely stationary. In the recent past our Earth's climate has been subjected to the Roman Warm Period (RWP, AD100-AD400), The Medieval Warm Period (MWP, AD 950 – AD 1250) and the Little Ice Age (LIA, AD1300 – AD1915)

- There are many possible contributors to the changes in the Earth's climate. These need further, unbiased study by balanced scientists who investigate matters that have not yet been tapped. For instance, to name only a couple of issues that have received little attention, how does the output of CO2 from the Earth's population of 7.6 billion people and the animals that feed them, work for them and are their responsibilities, compare with the CO2 produced by the production of electrical power? What is the output of CO2 from humanity's use of transport – its ships, its aeroplanes and its land vehicles? Can an accurate measure of these important amounts be arrived at and compared with the production of CO2 from natural sources such as volcanoes and the destruction of old forests?

Unless an investigation shows that sources of CO2, other than the production of electricity, produce far less CO2 than that produced by the making of electricity by burning coal, we might be making a giant mistake in abandoning electrical power produced by burning coal.

- According to most sources Australia is responsible for only a small 1.3 – 1.4% of the Earth's production of CO2. Therefore what Australia does to cut its production of CO2 will have almost no effect. Unless China, the USA, Europe and India can find ways of producing their energy requirements that do not produce CO2, what Australia does is almost irrelevant.

- According to a letter published in *The Australian* newspaper on 10 August 2022 the number of electrical power plants in use, and proposed by various countries in the near future, is;
    - The EU – 27 new plants for a total of 495.
    - China – 1171 new plants for a total of 3534
    - Japan – 45 new plants for a total of 135
    - India – 446 new plants for a total of 1035
    - Australia – no new plants and is closing down its 6 existing plants. If these figures are correct what Australia is doing, in a juvenile attempt to prevent global warming, is ridiculous, especially in view of the fact that Australia is supplying coal to both India and China.

- Water vapour is, evidently, responsible for a greater "greenhouse effect" than CO2, yet it is not discussed as a major contributor. Why not? Is it because humanity cannot be held responsible for

the greenhouse effect of water vapour? Why is the IPCC not attempting to control water vapour as it is currently trying to control the production of CO_2 by humans?
- If humanity is to become really serious about reducing its production of CO_2, it will need to reduce its wasteful modes of living, its use of carbon rich fuel driven air, land and sea transports, and its current means of producing electricity, or it must find a means of producing electrical power that is free of CO_2. Australia, and the rest of the world, will need to rethink their objections to the production of electrical power by nuclear fission and perhaps we will need to even consider how we can reduce the number of humans living on our Earth and the number of animals that support them.
- "Renewable" energy producers – wind, wave action and solar – all require quite major structures and battery storage for peak usage. They require maintenance and cannot be turned on and off to suit demand, and they depend for their production on climate conditions that, as Europe has found in 2021, cannot be controlled by us humans. Structures for wind towers, according to the Wall Street Journal of the 5th, of August 2019, each require 900 tons of steel, 2500 tons of concrete and 45 tons of plastic. What is the energy return period for such a massive amount of energy absorbing material? How long is it before a tower produces the energy required to make it, build it and maintain it? What is to be done with the towers when they have reached the ends of their useful lives?

These are absolutely basic questions that must be asked and answered before committing further to wind tower produced electrical power. I have not been able to find any readily available energy return figures for wind towers. Why not? It is a basic matter that should govern whether or not wind towers are practicable. Germany has been reported to be now pulling down more wind towers than it is now erecting. Then there is the matter of solar panels and their effectiveness. They also require huge amounts of concrete, steel, aluminium and glass. How long will they perform well?

Generally they are assumed to have a life of 25 years. What is to be done with their remains when they have used their useful lives? Are they recyclable? How can they be dealt with economically? And then there are the massive batteries that are required and that also have limited lives. Their used remains, which are toxic, will have to be disposed of. These are questions that need answering before the world commits to "renewables" further. What are the limits of their lives? How toxic are the remains of the batteries?

- The questions as to how the remains of solar panels and wind towers are to be dealt with after they have reached the ends of their useful lives and what are the lengths of those lives are questions that must be agreed and answered before there is more commitment to what might be future eyesores and inefficient users of arable land.

Before investing even more heavily in "renewables" the Energy Return on Energy Invested (EREI) of these systems should be ascertained. There are now enough photovoltaic (PV) installations, wind towers and wave grids, and they have been operating for long enough, for their life cycle costs (their EREI) and their power outputs over their useful lives to be measured, understood and compared to the energy used in their manufacture, erection, maintenance and disposal.

What is to be done with the residue of these power production systems when they are no longer capable of producing their power? Will their towers remain as boat and fish traps, as eyesores and bird traps and will the PV areas remain as shade houses on useful land on which they have been placed, or will they be disposed of? How will they need to be disposed of and at what cost of money and energy?

- Will large land areas of solar panels at higher latitudes – especially those in the northern hemisphere – be able to provide reliable supplies of electrical power during their long winter months, or will renewable energy supplies be forced to rely on the vagaries of wind?

Should humanity be attempting to lessen its impact by reducing its numbers? It is currently growing by approximately 80 million each year – mainly in Africa and southern Asia. Is it possible that our earth is already over populated?

Humanity must now realise that its different ethnic and religious groups have no alternative but to co-exist – to live together. Tribal squabbles have to be buried or all will be harmed. From a killing war no one will benefit. Humanity must learn to live in peace, and within the productive capacity of our globe. It must work towards peacefully living together or it will destroy itself. Its present actions of preparing for dangerous international conflicts is the height of foolishness.

There are really no easy alternatives for humanity if it is to thrive. It must recognise that war is now too destructive, and that the effects of nuclear warfare will be too long lived for a no holds barred war to be of benefit to anyone, even the survivors. It must also realise that the different parts of humanity have different characteristics, different beliefs and different moral codes, and that allowances have to be made for those differences.

Global warming, as put forward by the IPCC, is certainly a possibility, as is global cooling, as happened in the recent past in the Little Ice Age. For humanity to thrive, regardless of what nature throws at us, it must put its best hands and minds to work countering the new conditions as they arise. Humanity must abandon its squabbles, especially its arming for "defence". We all live on a fragile globe, and it needs our full attention. There are big decisions to be made and these must be formed by cooperation of, at least, a majority of the more powerful countries. Some of those decisions are:

- The optimum human population of our limited planet. The number depends on our Earth's capacity to produce food, shelter and worthwhile occupations. How can that figure be found and, once determined, how can it be achieved?
- What must humanity do to provide reasonable living conditions for a stable human population? Currently many people are either too hot or too cold, are suffering from a lack of food or are overeating, are suffering from curable and incurable diseases, and are fighting or arming for wars. Is this the best that humanity can offer?
- What do we have to do to protect ourselves from dangerous and incurable diseases? How can we maintain healthy populations that exercise and eat sensibly?
- What is the best way to provide balanced education for the young and for those who wish to increase their knowledge and understanding? Are schools and universities the optimum way of providing education? Will balanced, universal education solve the problems and frictions between ethnic and religious groups? I believe it can, but if it fails to achieve peace what can be done to create a period during which problems can be tackled by a united front?

8. ANOTHER VIEW OF GLOBAL WARMING.

I have recently had studies, carried out by Freeman Dyson, brought to my attention. He was a physicist who spent most of his working life as a Professor at Princeton. He has also worked on nuclear reactors and on solid state physics. He was a Fellow of the American Physical Society and of the Royal Society of London, and has written a number of books on scientific matters. He was obviously a highly intelligent scientist who considered possibilities other than those being pursued by the mainstream.

Professor Dyson said he took pride in being a heretic. One of his statements is *"My first heresy says that all the fuss about global warming is grossly exaggerated."* He opposes what he describes as *"the holy brotherhood of climate model experts"* but admits he has no degree in meteorology. He has studied climate *"models"* and has found them to be *"unreliable"* and gives reasons why they are. I believe his papers are balanced.

He investigated experiments with plant life grown in enhanced levels of CO2. They have shown that the plants *"react very strongly to enhanced carbon dioxide"* and has found that it *"has a drastic effect on plants because it is the main food source for plants."* The climate specialists appear to have ignored this advantage of higher levels of CO_2 in the atmosphere, which could help to feed the Earth's burgeoning population.

Given that the livelihoods of the climate change experts depend on the findings of their research Dyson finds *"it is difficult for them to say 'there isn't a problem"* and that *"they have a tremendous vested interest in the problem being taken more seriously, as it is."*

Dyson points out that the people of Greenland love the fact that it is warming, and also that five times as many people die of cold as die of heat.

He discusses the rise in sea levels as follows. *"The most serious of all the (global warming) problems is the rising sea level but, there again, we have no evidence that this is due to climate change"* as *"It has been going on for 12,000 years"* and that *"It is not clear whether it has been accelerating or not"* in the last 50 years.

Dyson also comments on the experts who fail to take into consideration factors that could influence climate – factors such as clouds, dust in the air, the chemistry and biology of fields, farms and forests – and says, about their models that *"They do not begin to describe the world we live in."*

He says that if CO_2 is the prime cause of climate change, as so many climate experts believe, it is possible *"To stop the carbon in the atmosphere from increasing"* and that *"we only need to grow the biomass in the soil by one hundredth of an inch per year."* He reaches the conclusion that *"the problem of carbon dioxide in the atmosphere is a problem of land management."*

He recommends that the USA becomes environmentally virtuous by accumulating China's production of CO_2 in its top soil. I have no idea if this is possible, but if it is it should be pursued. If topsoil can be enhanced by encouraging the sequestration of CO_2 in it that should be done. If it is not being done why is it not being done?

He also attacks the issue from other directions. He says, *"the warming effect of CO_2 is strongest where it is cold and dry,"* and adds, *"and occurs mainly at night in mountainous regions."* Possibly in an effort to show balance he reports *"The warming is real, but it is mostly making cold places warmer."*

He reports on experiments with plants grown in CO2 enriched atmospheres. These experiments have shown that the plants, at the ends of their life cycles, *"cause an increased transfer of carbon from the atmosphere into top soil."* He says that there have been no attempts to measure the difference, but, as he says, the fact that there have been no attempts to measure the carbon sequestered in the top soil does not mean it is unimportant.

Being a structural engineer, and being, therefore, well removed from having any great understanding of climate science I cannot comment on the accuracy of Dyson's arguments and his findings, but I am certainly swayed by those findings. It is highly likely that if global warming is occurring it is caused, in varying degrees by a number of causes – variations in the sun's emissions, changes in the angle of the Earth's axis and its distance from the sun, changes in the amounts of dust and water vapour in the atmosphere, humankind's changes to the surfaces of our globe and our burning of massive amounts of fossil fuels. Whether the warming is a bad thing has yet to be ascertained – just ask the people of Greenland and consider the sad fate of Napoleon's army in Russia.

Because the major emitters of CO2 – China and India – are not committing to cutting their production of the gas, because burgeoning CO2 is, almost certainly, going to increase plant crops, and because areas such as Greenland are likely to become green and productive again, there is little point in Australia, or many other countries, giving their populations the high cost, interference with its land use and doubtful benefits of "renewables". Wind towers and solar panels take up areas that could be used for other, productive pursuits, and are enriching their makers – China.

As thoughtful and knowledgeable people, such as Freeman Dyson, doubt the efficacy of the current crop of energy producing "renewables", have doubts about the possible catastrophes arising out of using coal, gas and oil for creating civilisation's electrical power and its means of transport, and have considered the possible means of sequestering CO_2 into our soils to increase their fertility, I think we in Australia should not commit wholeheartedly to the "renewables" until it is certain that it is necessary to do so. If we wait until global heating is a certainty, and there are developed "renewables" industries, we will have the benefit of the development that will occur as the major emitters – China and India – also are driven to abandon fossil fuels.

9. COMPARING POSSIBLE FUTURE ELECTRICAL POWER SOURCES.

Between 360 and 300 million years ago, during the carboniferous period, and during the period between 145 and 66 million years ago, the cretaceous period, the verdant forests and ferns, the developing maritime creatures and planktons and the very large land creatures of that luxurious time lived and died and, with time and pressure, formed into the coal, oil and gas deposits that humanity is now harvesting. But can the burning of these fabulous deposits continue to warm humanity, provide modes of transport and energy of various types without any penalty, or does humanity have a price to pay for their use? In this section I discuss these matters without arriving at any firm conclusions.

I write this as a structural engineer who is attempting to make sense of the disagreements that cloud the selection of our future electrical power sources. The disagreements I have studied are often emotionally based, not intellectually based, and the arguments put forward by all sides are often based on figures that are quite different and ignore the global and long term pictures. Some are based on unknown future possibilities that might or might not become realities, some completely ignore what is to be done with the detritus from the system being espoused, and some imply that what is a universal matter (such as saving the Great Barrier Reef) can be solved by cutting Australia's 1.3% - 1.4% production of CO_2, which is obviously wrong. Only if the major emitters of CO_2 control their outputs will what Australia does matter. I will now outline the positions being taken by those who are greatly concerned about global warming and those who are ignoring the possibilities of a global crisis and are continuing to produce massive amounts of CO_2, and add comments I consider are relevant.

Those concerned about global warming take the position that "renewables" are the answer to the supply of electrical power, so humanity should be concentrating its efforts and its finances on them – wind, tidal and wave power, hydro power from dammed water and solar power. Except for hydro power production these are the means of providing electrical power championed by the "greens" in their efforts to save the globe. Of the "green" producers of electrical power only hydro has the ability to be controlled and not to require battery storage of power produced when conditions are favourable, but it has the possible disadvantage of changing the natural flow of rivers.

There is another possible saviour – hydrogen. As it burns it produces heat that can be used for industrial purposes and for making electricity. Its residue is pure water so that if it can be produced economically, and without requiring a great deal of energy, it would be ideal. Unfortunately there is, as yet, no way of producing pure hydrogen except by electrolysis, which separates water into its components – hydrogen and oxygen – and that requires electricity. Hydrogen is a very volatile material and, because it is the lightest of all the elements it is difficult to contain. It is also highly flammable as the Germans found out with the catastrophe of the Hindenburg zeppelin in 1937.

There are those humans and countries that are going to continue to burn fuels, stored near to the Earth's surface in ages past, because they consider that it is the most economical means of powering transport and producing electricity. There are also those who believe that a warming globe with a higher content of CO_2 in the atmosphere, could have advantages such as better growth of cereals, and other crops, and pleasanter climatic conditions for many of our current living animal and vegetable species, as occurred during the Roman Warm Period (100AD – 400AD) and the Medieval Warm Period (950AD – 1250AD). Those opposed to the production of CO_2 – who are certainly in the ascendant position at this time in the western world – argue that warming will adversely affect such assets as coral reefs and will cause sea levels to rise, forcing many peoples off their low lying island homes. They also consider that the warmer conditions will lead to more forest fires, to unpleasantly hot climatic conditions on much of the Earth's surface and to flooding.

The fact that there have been warmer and colder times during the short period of recorded history receives little attention. During the Roman Warm Period, grapes were grown in northern England. During the Medieval Warm Period, long before humanity started to burn the ancient fuels of coal and oil in big quantities, Eric the Red (950 – 1003) colonised Greenland, gave it its name, and grew crops there. The settlers were forced to leave when the Little Ice Age (1300 – 1915) made agriculture impossible. If there is now a rise in global temperature, Greenland could become green again and possibly climate changes could alter what are now desert areas and they could, once again, grow the vegetation that probably gave rise to the oil under Saudi Arabia.

Possible advantages from a warming climate, such as areas of the Earth's surface becoming warm and wet enough to support crops and people, areas that are now of little use to humanity, are rarely raised. There are claims, especially by the greens and the IPCC (the Intergovernmental Panel on Climate Change) that the science is settled. On the evidence now available that does not appear to be so. We will see.

I have looked with interest at the short term climate forecast of Europe on the internet. Humans have now been burning fossil fuels since early in the 19th century, so the amount of CO_2 in our Earth's atmosphere has reached levels higher than they have been for 3 million years (this figure came from charts published on the internet). According to the IPCC, this is causing a sharp rise in the Earth's temperature. However, if we look at the winter forecasts for Europe in 2022 by the expert meteorologist Tyler Roys there are surprises. He says, *"Temperatures during the second half of winter will dip to near normal and below normal levels over north western Europe"* and *"On top of chilly winds out of the east the La Nina phase will increase the opportunity for snow across the United Kingdom and Ireland as well as areas from France to Poland, especially later in the season."* It is difficult for me, an engineer, to accept that a late icy winter over much of Europe, which incidentally did occur, equates to global warming unless there are balancing heat bursts over other parts of the globe. If global warming is occurring, perhaps it should be welcomed.

The Tyler Roys' predictions have had support. In *The Australian* on 23 April 2008 Phil Chapman wrote an article that suggested an ice age was coming because of a lack of sun spots. In it he pointed out that 2007 was exceptionally cold and that it had snowed in Baghdad for the first time in centuries. He did make the point that this did not prove another little ice age was coming but he put forward a case for preparing for an ice age that would reduce food supplies on the basis that *"The next descent into an ice age is inevitable."*

What is clear is that the IPCC's claim that the science is settled, and that our Earth is going to heat up due to our production of CO_2, is not necessarily what the future holds for humanity, and that, based on history and the living conditions during the Roman Warm Period and the Medieval Warm Period, warming periods would appear to be preferable to another ice age.

I have attempted to get a clearer understanding of the Energy Return on Energy Invested (EREI) of the possible producers of electrical energy. What I have found is that figures produced by investigators are often obscure and always diverse. Most investigators appear to be in favour of systems that produce electrical energy from wind and solar but are not in favour of electrical power produced by burning hydro-carbons or by nuclear fission or nuclear fusion. There are those who favour hydro power because it can meet demands, and provide useful water sources, and those who object to altering the natural flows of rivers. There are now studies being undertaken on Life Cycle Assessments (LCAs) which could provide clearer pictures and evidence as to the direction humanity should go in its search for its growing electrical power requirements.

Whatever happens, it is clear that humanity will want more and more electricity as less developed countries develop and as traffic of all types turns more and more to electrically powered vehicles. There is a source of electrical power that is fairly recent, appears to be economical and is almost CO2 free. It is nuclear power. Although it appears to be providing over 70% of Frances electrical power, peacefully and without problems, it is still regarded with suspicion by Australian governments and by those in favour of renewables – who might have financial interests in those renewables.

I now record my thoughts on the pros and cons of the various possible electrical power producers, and look forward to getting the thoughts of others, and criticisms for statements I have made when I have not managed to be balanced.

Wind power – The prime advantage of electrical power produced from wind towers is that it does not result in the production of any CO2 once the towers, their foundations, their batteries and their necessary distribution systems are established, except for maintenance.

The building of the towers, their foundations, their large fans, their necessary back-up battery systems and their maintenance absorb a good deal of energy, but this has often been ignored by their proponents. Why the energy needed to produce "green" systems has not been widely compared with the outputs of those systems, and has not been the major point of discussion and investigation I do not understand. A fundamental requirement of any system for the production of electricity is that it produces more electricity than was required for its production. This absolutely basic requirement seems to be largely ignored by the enthusiasts for "green" energy. It is rarely discussed.

In August 2015 the Wall Street Journal printed an article entitled *"If You Want Renewable Energy Get Ready To Pay."* The article pointed out that one wind turbine requires 500 tons of steel, 2500 tons of concrete and 45 tons of non-recyclable plastic. How much energy goes into making such a major machine was not discussed and there was no estimate of how long such a tower will take to replace the energy that went into making it and its supporting batteries, or how long the towers will be productive. What was provided was that dismantling de-commissioned towers, after they had reached the ends of their useful lives, would generate millions of tons of waste. I have found no investigations of the lives of typical wind turbines and their battery systems, but the estimate of such lives appears to be 20 years to 25 years. The article also pointed out that solar panels – the alternative "green" electricity producers require even more concrete, steel and glass – and rare earth elements – than wind towers.

Is the world being sold a false saving of our Earth by those selling these alternative producers of electrical power? Until there are unbiased analyses of how long towers, and their supporting batteries, take to create the power that goes into making and maintaining them, there is no basis for our world to build more of these towers that do not improve the landscape, that produce unpleasant noises and that are dangers to bats and birds. There have been several structural failures of wind towers and I understand that Germany is now pulling down more wind towers than it is building.

Electricity produced by wind appears to have other shortcomings. The main one is that it is not normally available to meet demands so it must be stored for those high demand periods, which adds to its cost. Electricity generated by wind power cannot be turned up and down to suit demand, so it has to be stored to meet high demand periods. Also it is dependent on the wind blowing, as Germany found out during its winter of 2021-2022.

Being machines, wind towers not only need maintenance, they will also wear out with time and use, and cease functioning efficiently. There have been several wind towers that have failed structurally, and many that have failed mechanically. On a trip through Germany in 2015 I saw that as many as 1 tower in 10 was not working.

I have no personal experience as to how long wind towers will operate before they need to be replaced and what will have to be done to dispose of their carcasses once they have worn out. I also do not know, although I have asked an engineer who has installed them, how long a wind tower takes to return the energy required to make and install it, and to provide the batteries necessary to provide continuous electrical power from that form of "clean" electrical power. I did not get a clear answer. If the energy return period is short I believe that it would be widely advertised. As its energy return period is not being widely broadcast it is probable that it is not a complete success story.

There is also the matter of the cost of the electrical power wind towers produce. According to an article that was in *The West Australian* on 14 June 2006, the cost of power produced by wind is almost twice the cost of power produced by coal. There are, of course, other costs than production costs, such as the costs of power storage, and figures can be produced that attempt to justify the added costs of renewables, such as estimates of the possible costs of global warming.

As I write this in the month of November 2021, at the beginning of the northern hemisphere's winter there is a shortage of electrical power, and its cost, in Europe, is spiraling up partially because the wind is not blowing. That wind power cannot be controlled to meet demand and needs expensive storage is a major drawback.

Wind towers are large structures that do not appeal to everybody, they need to be placed where they will receive wind and they produce noises that some find objectionable. They need very large concrete footings to stabilise them, and high quality materials in their shafts and their wind blades. They also need banks of batteries to store excess power being generated during peak wind times, to be distributed during high demand periods, and DC/AC converters.

To make, install and maintain wind towers requires a good deal of energy. The questions that need to be answered are – how long does a tower have to operate before it returns the energy required to make and maintain it, how long will a tower last before it is decommissioned, and what is to be done with the remains once the towers have lived their useful lives?

Wind power does not appear to be a reliable supplier, or to be capable of being the main provider of electricity for any large housing area, and especially for industrial use. With its reliance on fickle wind it appears that all it can be called on to do is act as a fringe supplier, and then only if it can be shown that it is economical.

Tidal and wave power – Tidal and wave power producers have not received as much attention from the renewables world as wind and solar power producers have. Why is unclear, because, as water is much denser than air, the energy producers do not have to be so large, expensive and intrusive. Tidal and wave power producers are, of course, separate forms of using the ocean to generate electrical power

Tidal energy producers require high tidal rises and falls so they can only be used in locations that have such tides. Their prime advantages are that they are reliable – there will be tidal rises and falls as long as the moon circles the Earth – and they can produce power from both incoming and outgoing tides. The machinery that is necessary is robust and long lived even in saline conditions. Their disadvantages to date have been their high initial cost and that they could affect the sea environments in which they operate

– disadvantages tidal power shares with dams for hydro power and towers for wind power. They need to be made from materials that can withstand saline conditions.

There is a possibility that future developments will reduce the cost of tidal energy and make it environmentally safer, as new approaches to harvesting it are found. At this time tidal power is a limited possibility for supplying the electricity necessary for operating human industries and habitations, as it is only viable in high tidal movement areas, which are limited, and it shares the other renewables shortcoming that the power produced has to be stored. It might be possible for tidal power to be used to produce hydrogen economically and to use the hydrogen produced to then produce electricity where it is required.

There has been a good deal of experimentation with wave production of electrical energy. Wave energy is a product of the energy inherent in wind, so it is only available when the wind is blowing. Capturing the energy of sea swells and waves in a manner that is useful and economical has not yet been accomplished. Different methods of capturing and utilising wave energy have been tried. So far none have been found to be effective and economical. Experimentation is still being carried out so that it is possible that an economical conversion method will be found. At this time wave energy is an unlikely replacement for the electrical energy now provided by coal and gas.

Hydro power – Deriving power from water trapped behind dams is an economical method of producing power and it has the added advantages of providing water for human consumption, for irrigation and for flood control during high rain periods. It has the downsides that it is dependent on rainfall, it does change the environment, and it can only be used where the topographical features are suitable. It requires relatively narrow valleys. Where hydro power can be used in the future it should be used, as it is being used in China and in Tasmania. Hydro has the added virtue of being able to be partially restored during low load times by pumping water back using spare electricity.

Solar power – Solar power is now available in two forms. It is used for individual buildings as panels on their roofs and walls, and it is used as panel farms that take up land areas that could possibly be used for other purposes. Solar power from roof panels is popular in Australia for residences – but is it because it is efficient and economical, or is it because the government is making it attractive by subsidising it? In the USA the cost of an 8 kWh system for a house is in the region of $USD18,000. In Australia the cost in Australian dollars is less than half that. Why is there such a difference? Is it because the government is hiding the true cost of solar electricity by subsidising it? If it is, why is it doing that? Surely when alternative power sources are being compared they should be compared on a similar basis.

In a paper, written by Rhianna King and published in The West Australian on 14 June 2006, she wrote that the cost of solar power was 50c to $1 per kWh. This compared, most unfavourably, with coal (4.7c – 9c), nuclear (3.9c) and hydro (2c – 5c). How she established her figures I have no idea but if they are accurate it means that solar panels – panels that lose efficiency with age and have to be dismantled and stored somewhere or re-cycled at the ends of their useful lives – are not the answer they have been made out to be by their purveyors. I note that there are those who believe that solar power in the USA will be produced for as little as 3c per kWh. Before this low figure becomes the figure that is used for comparisons, the costs of establishing the solar panels and their supporting battery systems and then removing both at the ends of their useful lives and recycling them or storing them permanently, should be taken into account.

Then there are the necessary, large panel farm areas. The fields they need to cover to absorb the necessary sunlight for producing power on a large scale, are precluded from supporting any form of habitation or industrial use. Areas they occupy can, possibly, be used for growing stock feed or vegetables by leaving spaces between the panels. Perhaps Australia with its wide open spaces of semi-desert could be used for panel farms but other countries might find that they are taking up arable areas or desirable living spaces.

Production of electricity by solar panels shares another drawback with wind power and wave power in that it is not available on demand. Electricity can only be produced during daylight hours and its availability is subject to weather conditions and hours of sunlight, so it needs storage, or a back-up system, to be available for times of peak demand and for the hours when the sun is not shining because of short periods of sunshine during winter in areas of high latitudes, or is affected by storms.

Solar power does not appear to be a balanced source of electrical power in its existing form. Its proponents have made a success of selling it in Australia, but it is obviously not suitable as a winter power source in areas of high latitude (such as northern Europe, Canada and much of Russia) where short periods of sunshine are experienced during the high demand periods of winter. In these areas there will continue to be a requirement for a reliable source of electrical power to provide the necessary domestic heating, lighting and power and power for industrial use.

In time it might be possible to store the energy accumulated by the long periods of sunshine that the high latitudes receive during their summers but without an efficient storage system being developed solar power is obviously of limited widespread use.

Coal, oil and gas power – Coal, oil and gas are fossil fuels that were laid down in the Carboniferous period over 300 million years ago. Humanity learned to harness steam energy from burning fossil fuels in the latter half of the 18th century, when steam engines were developed and used to power trains and ships. Then, late in the 19th century, the internal combustion engine was developed and used to power cars, and later other forms of transport. The world is currently reliant on fossil fuel burning vehicles, including ships and aeroplanes.

Now there is a thrust to do away with using fossil fuels as sources of power because burning them produces carbon dioxide (CO_2). Currently there is a belief that the small amount of CO_2 in the atmosphere (approximately 400 parts per million) is causing the Earth to heat up and that this would be a catastrophe. How big a catastrophe it would be and when it will occur has not yet been established. The world has recently been exposed to previous warm periods (the Roman Warm Period (AD 100 – 400) and the Medieval Warm Period (AD 950 – 1250), which was followed by the Little Ice Age (AD 1300 – 1915) and about which little has been reported by the IPCC.

Australia should not be closing down its use of coal to provide electrical energy until others on our limited Earth stop using it to produce their electrical power. If the list of coal consumers below (sourced from *Global Coal Planet Tracker, Coalswarm, Platts, WEPP*) is correct, for Australia to stop using its plentiful supply of high quality coal when others are using it in much greater quantities and are also burning lower quality coal, seems quixotically foolish.

Place	Coal plants	New*	Total
EU	468	27	495
Turkey	56	93	149
South Africa	79	24	103
India	589	446	1035
Philippines	19	60	79
South Korea	58	26	84
Japan	90	45	135
China	2363	1171	3534
Totals	3722	1892	5614

Australia is planning to shut down its remaining plants in order to save the world!
*Under construction or recently completed

My own view is that humanity, and especially Australia, should not be too precipitate in doing away with fossil fuels until there is no doubt that CO_2 is the only, or at least the main, cause of any present warming period. The contribution of water vapour needs more consideration as do other possible warming contributors. (See *8. ANOTHER VIEW OF GLOBAL WARMING*). I also think that Australia should be very careful about upsetting its economy by abandoning fossil fuels before economical substitutes are agreed. Australia's contribution of CO_2 is small when compared with much larger emitters such as the USA, China, Russia and India who, with the exception of the USA, are not, currently, curbing their use of fossil fuels. Our output of CO_2 per head of population is certainly high because we live on a wide, brown land much of which needs warming in winter and cooling in summer, and which needs transport over distances.

Global warming is now an emotional issue – it has not been proven and the recent temperature rise prognoses have not been accurate. Australia should be preparing for both heating and cooling, but it should not destroy its economy until there is proof that cutting back humanity's use of fossil fuels will solve the global warming problem, if there is one, and the major emitters also agree to reducing their outputs of the gas.

Geothermal heat – Although it does not appear to be considered as a likely source of the heat humanity needs on our Earth's surface, there is a source available in abundance beneath our feet. Our Earth is a giant ball with a core that is, evidently, at a temperature of over 5000 degrees. Occasionally the outer layers of this heated core erupt through fractures in the Earth's solid mantle as volcanoes and geysers. If the heat of this core could be tapped and used, humanity would almost certainly have a sufficient heat source to see out its tenure on Earth without unduly interfering with the heat balance of the globe. The problem is – how do we safely, economically and efficiently trap and use that heat? Current attempts have generally been too expensive and raise the question of the possibilities of starting uncontrollable lava leakages that could be destructive. Perhaps, in the future, humanity will devise a safe and economical means of tapping the heat, using it and controlling it. Obviously handling the high temperature of the core would be a tremendous problem but we would only need temperatures of something over 100 degrees to operate our machinery and to provide warmth for humanity.

Currently Iceland leads the world in its use of geothermal heat, using it to warm the majority of its houses and for industrial purposes. It produces 73% of its electricity from hydro power and 27% is geothermally produced. Because it has access to economical electrical power, and despite the fact that it has no direct access to bauxite, approximately half of Iceland's production of electrical power is used for producing aluminium because its electrical power is cheap.

Power from hydrogen – When hydrogen burns it produces heat and its residue is only pure water. Therefore it would appear to be the best answer to the world's energy shortages, but there are both positives and problems. It is light in weight which would be an advantage for fueling aircraft. Being extremely volatile it is difficult to store and transport safely, and without loss.

Currently its cost of production is very high and unless the cost of electrolysis can be reduced it will not replace other forms of energy. It must be stored under high pressure, its storage must be reliably leak proof, and it is difficult to transport, especially in large quantities.

If hydrogen is to be our fuel of the future it will require a great deal of development. I have not seen an analysis of the energy required to produce, liquefy and store hydrogen, which compared that to its energy output when burnt. This comparison should be widely available as it either shows that hydrogen is the answer to future power production or that it is not. In our present state of knowledge it looks as though all hydrogen will be is a fringe supplier of energy.

Nuclear power – Australia, and a good percentage of the world's more advanced economies, appear to be sharply divided about the production of electricity by nuclear power. There are those concerned about the safety aspects experienced by the fission power plants of Three Mile Island, Fukushima and Chernobyl, and those who have a belief in "renewables" as the providers of electrical power in the future. Some are concerned that the products of the nuclear fission reactions are so dangerous for so long that they should not be considered as a power source.

Then there are those who point to France, now largely dependent on electrical power produced by nuclear fission for domestic and industrial use, and on nuclear fission powered submarines for defence, both of which have, so far, excellent safety records. Electricity produced by nuclear fission does not need the large power storages that are required by the "renewables" because its outputs can be readily adjusted, and are not subject to the vagaries of nature, as is power produced by wind and solar.

What is clear is that production of steam by harnessing the heat produced by nuclear fission, which is then used to create electrical power, is an economical, reliable and controllable method of producing electricity. What is also clear is that the lessons from failures of nuclear plants in the past have now been learnt and are extremely unlikely to be repeated.

The main concern with the production of electricity by nuclear fission is that the waste from that production is highly radioactive, is hazardous to humans, and it has a life of thousands of years. This is being dealt with by burying the used uranium deeply in remote locations (of which Australia has an abundance) but it is still a concern.

Nuclear fusion also produces great amounts of energy, and it leaves a much more stable residue. Fusion has not yet received the attention that fission has. Once the reactions of fusion can be controlled, it might replace fission because its residue is much more benign. Time and science might result in fusion being the world's electrical power provider in the future. There are several groups working on experimental fusion approaches.

Another concern about using nuclear reactions is that the time taken to design and construct a nuclear power station is considerable. In my view Australia should be planning for nuclear power now even if humanity finds, in time, that burning fossil fuels is safe and even benefits humanity's food crops, because energy derived from uranium and thorium is economical and controllable.

There are obviously costs attributable to nuclear power that must be considered, such as the prices of the buildings housing the reactors, which are expensive, the cost of safely housing the highly radioactive remains the process leaves, and the dismantling and storing of the nuclear power plants once they reach the ends of their useful lives.

Some sources of power that are not fossil fuels or nuclear are being utilised and refined – wind, solar and wave. The main shortcoming with these alternative sources of energy is that they do not respond to demand, especially during periods of night, or low sunlight, so power must be stored. Also they are reliant on wind and sunshine, which are not reliable, especially during winter periods in northern and southern areas of the globe. Electrical power produced by tidal power is reliable, but it can only be economically tapped at limited sites, and it cannot react to demand unless it is also stored. The only reliable "green" source that can provide power on demand is hydro and it can only work efficiently at limited sites.

Apart from fossil fuels – coal, oil and gas – only hydro and nuclear are currently able to produce power on demand and hydro is heavily dependent on topography.

Western governments are attempting to reduce the output of the "greenhouse" gases, CO_2 and methane. Until now the approach to this reduction has mostly been to replace fossil fuels with "renewables" over a period of years. During the period this replacement has taken, and is still taking, place it will be possible to get a more exact assessment as to whether or not the Earth's temperature is rising catastrophically, as many now believe is occurring, or whether the rise in temperature and the increase in CO_2 in the atmosphere will lead to more luxuriant growth and some areas, such as Greenland, becoming green again. Humanity will have the opportunity to assess whether the warming, which will probably occur, will be beneficial or disastrous.

If the temperature does rise and the rise does lead to problems, then it could be necessary to produce basic electrical power by nuclear means or to learn how to sequester CO_2 in topsoil. If the temperature does rise, and the rise proves to be beneficial, all will be well. Time will tell. Humanity should prepare for both rising temperatures and for temperatures that decline. My own view is that we should be developing nuclear electrical power backed by tidal, hydro and renewables where appropriate, and phasing out fossil fuels. It is not a view shared by most of the Earth's governing bodies.

10. FUTURE AIMS FOR HUMANITY.

If our Earth is going to be able to support its huge range of plant growths and animals in a peaceful and productive way, which should be humanity's aim, it appears to me that several changes should be made.

- I repeat what I have written previously. I regard, as probably the most important action of humanity, that the young be educated in a balanced and comprehensive manner, free from the doctrines that have led to the stupidities of armed conflicts in the past.

  This will not be easy to achieve as most of the present crop of "leaders" do not have peaceful endeavours and cooperation as their driving forces. Their aims appear to be increasing their own importance and the power of the section of humanity that they lead. They appear ready to sacrifice their armies to achieve greater power. Unless the young of all colours and creeds learn from balanced teachers, (both their parents and their school teachers) in a balanced way, with no religious bigotry and no distortions of history, there is no chance of humanity achieving balanced calm, universal cooperation, enduring peace, and fulfilment of humanities' potentials. Perhaps peace and development is not what humanity really wants! Does a large and leading section of humanity enjoy wars and the killing of enemies? If they do – why do they? Is beneficial development not better than destruction?

- The able bodied and able minded must learn that it is their duty to serve their total human society – not just their religious or racial affiliates – and, especially, not just their own pockets. They must learn that it is their duty to provide value when they serve their society.

Although what I am calling for is possibly unachievable for all persons living in their various societies, the principle of teaching ethical and serving behaviour to the young is sound, and should be followed. All people should be encouraged to understand that their society is more important than their own position in that society, and their own share of the wealth of their society, when they conduct their businesses and their professional duties.

The situation in societies in which many attempt to maximise their own financial positions, often by means that are morally doubtful, does not result in societies that are peacefully productive, which should be the aim of any society. Successfully serving their society is any citizen's own, and principal, reward.

- Political decisions should be made based on a premise of the most good for the most people those decisions affect, not on the basis of how many votes will be attracted at the next election. Political leadership should be given to balanced, thoughtful and knowledgeable individuals who accept their positions as duties to their society – not as staffs of power for them to wield. They should be driven by a wish to serve, not by a wish to wield power for its own sake, and not as a path to self-importance.

Will people who are qualified to act as leaders and who have a wish to serve stand, or will they prefer to work in less public positions? And if they do stand for office will their parties select them or will the party prefer more public figures such as Malcolm Turnbull and Julia Gillard?

- The pursuit of wealth for its own sake is not a virtue. Those who accumulate wealth should not be given civic awards unless they have earned them by serving society in some other way. If wealth is accumulated in an honourable way, is not the result of taking from the efforts of others and is used wisely for the benefit of society, it is admirable. If it is achieved at the cost of society or by overcharging, it is not admirable. Those who take wealth from their society to satisfy their ego or their greed, and there are many of those, give the pursuit of wealth a bad name.
- Although I have agreed that religions can be retained as they can provide hope, stimulus and contentment for their followers, for those religions that have, in the past encouraged, and still do encourage, forced enlistments in armed services, and that condone severe physical punishments and the killing of non-believers, I have no time.

  I consider the human race should abandon existing religions as many earlier religions have been abandoned in the past. If the young are educated in a balanced way, and the atrocities that have been carried out by various religious groups in the past (and even to the present time) are explained in a balanced manner, it is likely that the religions, as we now know them, will decline in importance and influence. I certainly hope that the religions that encourage forceful proselytization of unwilling acolytes and that instill a belief in their followers of a comfortable and eternal life after death, will fade out as humanity becomes united and peaceful, and uses its energies – both its physical and mental energies – to increase its knowledge, to build a better, safer and peaceful world, and to solve the many mysteries of our Earth and of limitless space.
- There needs to be a thorough and balanced investigation of the capacities of our Earth to support its populations of animals,

plants and humans. Having established what the capacities are – and that is going to be an Herculean task – we need to establish a means of not exceeding those capacities. It is unlikely that the findings, whatever they are, will be agreed to by the different racial, ethnic and religious groups, but having long term targets, and alerting humanity to the problems of overcrowding, will be worthwhile. The alternative is for uncontrolled growth of some groups and the decline of others, which is now happening. The findings will, almost certainly, lead to conflict between some groups, which is now also happening. Escalation of these destructive possibilities must be avoided if possible. The aim must be peaceful balance.

- One completely out of control product of humanity is garbage. Prior to humans being able to control fire and, from that, how to manufacture things, the detritus produced by the human, animal and vegetable inhabitants of our globe was organically recyclable and there was a balance as discarded materials quickly became absorbed back into the sources from which they came. Then humans, who were increasing in number, discovered how to control fire and with that discovery how to manufacture buildings, articles and machines that are long lived but which lose their usefulness as they age. Humanity now produces huge amounts of garbage – metals, fabrics, plastics, glass, paper, rubber and some timber items – that do not readily decompose and get absorbed back into the soils from which they came. The result is garbage, much of which is almost indestructible. How can humanity return to lifestyles that do not produce long-lasting garbage and still maintain high standards of living? This should be one of the leading aims of humanity.

- Another question I have often asked myself is – why do humans squabble – especially why do they squabble to a level at which they kill and wound each other? Of what advantage to humanity is arguing, fighting and killing? Is there some sensible background to the violent disagreements that have taken place since the dawn of humanity's appearance on planet Earth? Why have there been so many wars? Today countries are preparing for war, under the banner of "defence". What is the attraction of killing or being killed? Is it nature's way of controlling the number of humans? I understand disagreements and that different conclusions can be reached as problems are studied, but I do not understand why these disagreements can morph into violent conflicts instead of being settled as evidence, one way or another, is discovered. If humanity is going to continue to be the dominant species on Earth it has to learn to settle its differences in a less destructive manner than by armed conflict. Surely there are enough problems to solve, enough mysteries to pursue, enough discoveries to make and enough challenges to take on without humans warring and killing each other? I hope so.

There are many more challenges to humanity's intellect and inventiveness that will arise as we gain knowledge and understand more of our world and our universe. One thing that we humans will have to accept is that we are not supremely important and that a supreme God did not create us – we created him, her or it. There will be no God looking after us in a warm and comfortable after life once we die. Each of us gets only one life, and we are obliged to make the most of that one life. Some find satisfaction in using their one life to accumulate wealth and power, some in being domineering and some in serving and contributing to their societies. Most of us has to make a decision as to which God they will serve, except for those who die young or who are mentally or physically impaired.

The most important use of our lives is to continue to attempt to find positive reasons for living and serving our societies and our fellow human beings.

11. QUESTIONS FOR OUR TIME.

There are many questions that arise out of the political, religious, financial and moral states of the various populations of our Earth. A current, acute sore is the sad situation in Ukraine, which has been attacked. It has been invaded by Russian troops who are ruining cities, destroying homes and killing innocents. There are questions that humanity, as a whole, needs to ask, and to then arrive at answers that are as unbiased and as balanced as possible. Some solutions will require changes by some groups of humans in their dealings with other religious, ethnic, racial and tribal groups. It is time for humanity to unite and to start living as one family – which it is – instead of having groups of humanity sniping at other groups, disliking each other, attempting to conquer other groups and subjecting the conquered to second class citizenships.

Humanity must now grow up and act as a united group or it could destroy the Earth on which it now lives, and terminally damage itself. The questions that follow need answering for future world peace, and the health, safety and prosperity of the humans who now inhabit our globe, and for those who follow. We humans should be aware of the effects of our actions and should attempt to act in ways that are not damaging to others.

- An immediate question for the world and Australia is – what are Russia's and China's aims and plans for the future? Both are acting in a manner that signals that armed conflict is possible in that future. Russia's armed invasion of the Ukraine shows its leadership under Vladimir Putin is prepared for armed conflict and the deaths of many. China is increasing its armed might and is showing the world its incredibly disciplined troops and its mighty rockets, its war vehicles and its fighter planes and war ships. It appears to be preparing for armed conflict. Part of its longer range planning appears to be to buy fealty from several of the world's less financially able countries by providing facilities for them and having them owe for those facilities. China is building in Africa and in the countries of the Pacific.
- How has China been able to be so financially successful in such a short period? How has it been able to build its cities whilst equipping and training its disciplined armed forces and financing buildings and facilities in foreign lands? It has exhibited great energy and productivity. An example of its productivity is its construction of currently fashionable wind turbines for the world. What is the secret of its remarkable and swift rise to its current, prominent position?
- There are other mysteries that are closer to home. How can China import iron ore, gas and coal from Australia and produce steel at a lower cost than it could be produced from the raw materials in Australia? The extra handling and shipping must add to the cost of the steel produced. And why is China prepared to pay for the materials at prices a good deal higher than their costs of production? Is it that China owns major shares in the companies that are making these profits from mining iron ore and coal? What percentage of the companies making these profits is actually secretly owned by Chinese interests?
- Why cannot the various groups of humanity who inhabit our small Earth – groups from the still quite primitive, but with

their own beliefs, sciences and arts, to advanced peoples with sophisticated arts, sciences and understandings – live on that Earth peacefully? What is the twist in human nature that causes humans to have murderous clashes that benefit only those who wish to dominate, who are prepared to have fellow humans killed to achieve that domination, and the manufacturers of their weapons?

- Those who pay most dearly for wars are not those who promote them, they are those who are killed or maimed. Can universal peace become the norm or is humanity doomed to conflict and killing with ever more sophisticated weapons?
- Why can humanity not work together to become peaceful, but competitive and civilised groups with complementary skills and knowledge? This primary question needs answers. Or are we humans heading on a path to self-destruction?
- How long will it be before the group that is losing a war, using normal weaponry, reverts to nuclear weapons – weapons that are incredibly destructive and that will adversely affect the Earth for many years?

Those making the decisions for their societies to go to war with the aim of domination, and those who arm the front line fighters, will not normally expose themselves to the dangers of combat, but in the event of a nuclear war no-one will be free of the shattered mess that will result.

- Such a conflict will cause great devastation and damage to the environment and will leave behind ruined works of we humans. How to prevent a nuclear conflict should be the prime quest at this time. Instead, leaders often flaunt their expensive and destructive weapons. Is humanity really that childish and banal? Can agreement be reached that nuclear weapons are to be safely disposed of or is humanity prepared to live with the threat of a nuclear war hanging over it?
- Why do certain human beings want to dominate others and

are prepared to wantonly kill to achieve their aims? Why does humanity produce people such as Attila the Hun, Napoleon Bonaparte, Benito Mussolini, Adolf Hitler, Joseph Stalin, Harry S. Truman (who authorised the first, and last, use of atomic weapons) and now Vladimir Putin. And why do those who will be the gun fodder follow such leaders instead of following peaceful leaders who aim at producing a better world for their followers? Is it that humans are naturally violently competitive and that war has, until now, been only an advanced game?

- Competitions of many types can bring out the best traits in humans, but there are some competitions that feed primary weaknesses of humans. Examples are blood sports, the worst of which is human warfare. Lesser evils, but evils nevertheless, are training animals and humans to kill and permanently damage opponents. I consider that blood sports pander to the worst side of humanity. I strongly approve of competition between humans who are reasonably, evenly matched but I consider blood sports have no place in today's societies.
- And I cannot see how the worst type of competition – armed conflicts between different groups of humans – can have any benefit for the humans involved – even the victors – except that it could be nature's way of controlling the rate of growth of the human race so that the Earth can sustain those who are left.
- If this doubtful thesis has any validity it is time that it was scrapped in favour of humans taking control of their own numbers. Surely peace and the development of our knowledge and our works of art and science is superior to war and destruction.
- What are the optimum human and animal populations of our limited globe? It is necessary that figures for these be established so that balance can be achieved. And there will be no reasons for wars that claim the territory of other groups.

- It is unlikely that agreement will be readily reached by the various ethnic, religious, racial and tribal groups, but it is necessary that systems and controls of numbers be established.
- Without control of numbers in the future, humanity could exceed our Earth's capacities, so that unless agreements are reached, the alternative could be annihilation of much of humanity by wars or famines.
- Having studied and decided what the optimum world population is, how to persuade mixed groups of humanity to comply with the limitations found is the next task, and it will either be accomplished by humanity uniting and agreeing or humanity will continue on its ridiculous route to widespread destruction.
- For continuing peace and development, a vital component is balanced education, delivered without the emotive palaver that is so often a part of religious education. I recognise that many Christians, Moslems, Jews and other religious denominations will object to the loss of their beliefs of a benevolent God.
- Moslems and Christians will not readily accept the loss of their belief of a safe and comfortable life after death, and Jews will not happily agree to the loss of their superiority, but I see no alternative but to begin to abandon these, and other religions, if humanity is to unite and work together.
- A driving force behind much of the warring between races has been religious differences. It is important that the education provided is broad and based on the best knowledge available, but the most important aspect is that there is no personal God and that all must behave reasonably to benefit humanity and themselves – because it is necessary for the future of the human race – not because they want to spend forever in paradise.
- There are many more challenges for the human race to face, apart from finding how to live in balance with nature and peacefully with our disparate groups of humans.
- They include the possibilities of space exploration and

colonisation of our moon and distant planets, gaining a greater understanding of our Earth, with its huge core of heat and the possibility of tapping into that core to reduce our reliance on fossil fuels, nuclear fission and nuclear fusion, exploring other planets with the aim of finding materials not readily available on Earth, and studying further the effect of $CO2$ on plant life to increase our crop percentages.

- It is quite ridiculous that humanity spends its mental energies and its intelligence on preparing for wars when they are destructive and benefit no-one, when there are so many other avenues for it to pursue. The Egyptians built their pyramids and Greece and Rome built their wonderful temples. Surely we can also build admirable edifices – edifices that will last for thousands of years – for those who come after us to admire and wonder about.
- We humans are aware of the many living things on our Earth – the animals, insects and plants – and, since we humans became sentient, we have been searching for a logical explanation as to why and how they, and we, came into being. There have been attempts to fill this void by several individuals, many beliefs have been put forward, and many religions developed.
- The very fact there are many competing religions almost certainly means that none are correct and all are constructs of us humans. Then there are the ages of the main religions. Homo sapiens has existed for approximately 200,000 years but the main religions are only approximately 2000 or less years old.
- Surely an all knowing God would not have waited for such an extended period to let Her, His or Its subjects know of Its existence and would have selected better ambassadors than Muhammad and Jesus Christ to spread the word.
- It is quite illogical that parts of Homo sapiens have allowed themselves to believe in an all-powerful, benign and loving Deity when that all powerful God has allowed mankind to get into such a mess of warring tribes, sects and religions.

- God has not only allowed different parts of humanity to kill, maim and conquer other parts of humanity but has actively encouraged the slaughter of wars, such as the Crusades, and has allowed the persecution of those who do not comply with the religion in charge.
- I cannot see how, based on the clear evidence, any of the religions can be taken seriously. They have outlived their time.

Our Earth is a wonderful place and we humans are its prime animal product. We have the responsibility to look after it, to nurture it and to damage it as little as possible. We are the first inhabitants that leave behind anything other than rotting corpses and ant hills. How are we meeting our responsibilities? By blowing things up with ever more sophisticated explosives!

Please humanity, think of the future and make decisions that will improve our Earth, not decisions that help destroy its surface and the creations of we humans.

www.ingramcontent.com/pod-product-compliance
Lightning Source LLC
Chambersburg PA
CBHW080401030426
42334CB00024B/2951